# NEARLY
# ONE
# WORLD

To Ken Paulson
— with thanks for
making it all possible,

Al Neuharth

ALSO BY ALLEN H. NEUHARTH

Confessions of an S.O.B.
World Power Up Close
Window on the World
Truly One Nation
Profiles of Power
Plain Talk Across the USA

# NEARLY ONE WORLD

—

## Allen H. Neuharth

with Jack Kelley
and Juan J. Walte

USA TODAY BOOKS

DOUBLEDAY

NEW YORK  LONDON  TORONTO  SYDNEY  AUCKLAND

Published by Doubleday, a division of
Bantam Doubleday Dell Publishing Group, Inc.
666 Fifth Avenue, New York, New York 10103

**Doubleday** and the portrayal of an anchor with a dolphin
are trademarks of Doubleday, a division of
Bantam Doubleday Dell Publishing Group, Inc.

Library of Congress Cataloging-in-Publication Data

Neuharth, Allen.
  Nearly one world.

   1. Civilization, Modern—1950–     . 2. Social
history—1970–     . 3. Social values—Cross-
cultural studies.   4. Interviews.   I. Kelley, Jack,
1960–     .  II. Walte, Juan.  III. Title.
CB428.N47   1989        909.82        89-7700
ISBN 0-385-26387-2

August 1989

First Edition

Traveling is fatal to prejudice, bigotry
and narrowmindedness.

MARK TWAIN
*The Innocents Abroad*
1869

# CONTENTS

NEARLY
ONE
WORLD

# Linked, But Not Yet United: An Introduction

I N early 1988, we pulled together a team of Gannett journalists and launched Jet-Capade: an eight-month, thirty-two-country, six-continent, 148,261-mile newsgathering journey.

The mission? To see how divided, or united, the world then was. We wanted to find out what the powerful and the poor—from Havana to Hanoi, from Moscow to Madrid, from Rio to Riyadh—were thinking: about their lives, their country, the USA, the world.

To get the answers, we decided to use good old-fashioned people-on-the-street interviews, supplemented by exclusive sessions with key world leaders. By the time it was over in September 1988, our two dozen reporters had talked with more than two thousand people of all races, religions, and cultures—and had private and exclusive interviews with thirty heads of countries. Our country-by-country reports appeared on thirty-one successive Fridays in *USA Today*.

What did we find? In many crucial ways, the Earth is becoming as small as it appears to orbiting astronauts and cosmonauts. Global communications, universal trends, and common aspirations are making us more alike than we are different.

Despite our rich diversity, we gradually are becoming nearly one world.

Sure, the differences among the peoples of the world are many. And apparent. And often challenging. There's a multitude of languages. Different religions. Different foods. Different customs. Different political systems. We came across them every day:

• In Havana, Cuba, the country's top Catholic official told us how he steers his church through the obstacles put up by Cuba's communist regime. "I never use the word 'adapt.' I prefer to say that in some way we have accepted reality, without violent confrontations," said Monsignor Carlos Manuel de Cespedes, fifty-one.

But for Indians, religion is as much a part of life as the air they breathe. "The whole country is religious," said Radha Krishan, fifty-five, a Hindu priest in New Delhi. "People are joining cults because they are trying to find something. . . . The ultimate aim is to get salvation."

• In Stockholm, Sweden, marriage seems to be going out of fashion. "Marriage doesn't even enter our minds. It's not in our vocabulary," explained Liliane Ronnholm, twenty-three, a restaurant manager who has lived with her boyfriend, Lars Eriksson, for a year.

But half a world away in Seoul, Korea, education student Kang So-young feels pressure to get married. "People here think there's something wrong with an unmarried woman past thirty," she told us.

• And in Nairobi, Kenya, Stanley Muburuti, thirty-five, the assistant restaurant manager at a major tourist hotel, told us: "The Italians, they want lots of bread. The French want wine. The Americans want ice water, what we call 'American champagne.' "

Each is an example of the world's diversity. A rich diversity. A diversity that makes us interesting. And yes, one that often results in misunderstanding—and conflict. But dwelling on problems and differences would have been a mistake. That's why we would have gone wrong only sticking with think tank experts' pat answers.

By talking to the world's real experts—the meek and the mighty, bankers and beggars, lawmakers and law breakers, preachers and teachers, students and shopkeepers—we quickly realized that more and more people are:

- Eating the same foods
- Reading the same books
- Watching the same movies
- Listening to the same music
- Enjoying the same sports
- Sharing the same dreams and drives

Much of the common ground comes from the global spread of U.S. pop culture—which has become everybody's culture. The Chinese are eating Kentucky Fried Chicken in Beijing. The Japanese are lining up to see Mickey at Tokyo's Disneyland. There's a McDonald's in Rome. And country music and rock 'n' roll can be heard virtually all over the world. It's a worldwide network of shared experience.

But there's more than that. Much more.

- We share history. World War II tore us apart. Killed at least forty million people around the world. Many of them were German relatives of mine. Others were infantry buddies in the U.S. Army's 86th Division. The scars and memories are still there. On both sides. Always will be. But the resulting desire to avoid bloodshed is also there. The dream of peace is a universal dream.

- We share technology. Communication satellites make it possible for millions to share the information and entertainment that's on television. Satellites also have revolutionized telephone and telefax communication. We sent reporters all over the world, but rarely were they out of reach of a telephone.

- We share high-speed transportation. Today, it takes less than twenty-four hours to travel between virtually any two points in the world. And it's all because of a very common piece of technology: the jet engine. That one device makes it possible for more of us to visit each other and to help each other. And, unfortunately, to hurt each other. Still, the jet engine, on a day-to-day basis, does more to bring us together than to push us apart.

I already had visited a number of the countries on our itinerary. Many of them more than once. Some of them forty years ago. Then the differences dividing the world were depressing. Today, the world really is coming closer to what Marshall McLuhan predicted twenty-five years ago: a global village. The countries of the world are now linked, although not yet united.

It may be unrealistic to suggest that we'll ever be truly united. But surely it's not foolish to work for it. And that's where journalists come in. It's our responsibility and opportunity to try to bring that about by reporting all the news: the good and the bad, the glad and the sad. What people want to know. And what people need to know. Around the world.

Beyond that we have a choice. We can either practice informational journalism or confrontational journalism. We can either inform, or indict and incite. It's the difference between promoting disunity or promoting unity.

How do journalists properly do this? It's simple. They must remain sensitive to different political systems and philosophies. They must report international issues from all perspectives. Not just their own. When journalists go out into the world, they must be worldly.

What follows is our attempt to tell about the world we found. Not the one we wanted to find. The purpose of Jet-Capade was to gain a better understanding; the purpose of this book is to convey that understanding to you—our readers. We have tried to do that with clear, unbiased communication.

In Piraeus, Greece, one of the "experts" we interviewed told us how important that is. He was Gregory Hadjieleftheriadis, a fifty-year-old international businessman.

"In the years to come," he said, "there are going to be no more wars, because of the wonderful miracle of communication."

# CHAPTER 1

# Popular Culture Is
# Born in the USA

U.S. pop culture has made its way into nearly all corners and
crevices of the world. Akiyo Otazawa, twenty-eight, and her
daughter Natsuki, one, waited in the hot morning sun at
Tokyo's Disneyland for a hug from their hero,
Mickey Mouse.

Photo: Callie Shell, *Nashville Tennessean*

ALMOST in the shadow of Chairman Mao's mausoleum in Beijing is a monument venerating another man—a foreigner wise in the ways of chickens.

He is the USA's Colonel Sanders. Founder of Kentucky Fried Chicken. Keeper of the secret blend of eleven herbs and spices. Guardian of the recipe for the "Colonel's famous gravy." Every day, more than a thousand Chinese file past the Colonel's plastic, life-size statue to sample his famous cuisine.

Beijing's Kentucky Fried Chicken restaurant is just like any KFC in Hometown, USA—only it's larger. In fact, it's the Colonel's biggest, according to twenty-eight-year-old general manager Sim Kay Soon. He's a Singapore citizen who has been in charge since the restaurant's grand opening in October 1987.

"We have three floors, we can seat

five hundred people at a time, and we use nine thousand chickens a week," Sim boasts.

How's business? KFC is selling enough to plan more restaurant outlets. With a population of more than one billion and an expanding standard of living, China is a dream come true for the fast-food business.

Is it cheap? Not really. Two dollars for a two-piece meal is a big bite out of the average monthly salary in China—$66. But it's fast.

A visitor from the USA would pick up on a couple of interesting differences:

There's no drive-through window, because most Chinese travel by bicycle or public transportation. And the closest translation in Chinese for "finger lickin' good" comes out "good enough to suck your fingers."

Otherwise, it is authentic USA fast food.

Line up.

Get it fast.

Eat it fast.

It also is an excellent example of the USA's No. 1 export: popular culture.

This popular culture consists of films and fads. Food and fashion. Rock and Rambo. Jazz and jeans. McDonald's and Mickey Mouse. You can flip on the radio just about anywhere in the world, and you're more likely to hear Motown than Mozart. The USA's pop culture has become a global culture. It's everybody's culture—from Cape Town to Tokyo.

• In Argentina, Tina Turner is a top rock star, and *Miami Division—Miami Vice,* in the USA—is a top TV program.

• In Saudi Arabia, Pepsi is the No. 1 packaged drink.

• In India, young men idolize Sylvester Stallone in *Rocky* and *Rambo,* while women work out at health clubs featuring Jane Fonda fitness tapes.

• In Singapore, *The Cosby Show* is big.

• In South Korea, Madonna is hot.

• In Paris, Bruce Springsteen is "The Boss"—just as in the USA. Just as in much of the world. Forty-five thousand people packed the Hippodrome on June 19, 1988, to hear him sing.

- In Poland, *CNN Headline News* broadcaster Bobbie Battista is a big celebrity.
- In Japan, there are more USA fast-food restaurants than in any country outside North America. McDonald's, Denny's, Wendy's, Dunkin' Donuts, Mister Donuts, Domino's Pizza, Häagen-Dazs shops. And more.
- Around the world, *Dallas* is considered the most widely watched TV show.

Nalini Mukherjee, forty-year-old deputy director of the Reserve Bank of India in Bombay, is proof of the intercontinental connection:

"We watch a lot of films on the VCR. We see your *Dallas* and *Dynasty* and *The Colbys.* When I went to Dallas, I visited the South Fork Ranch. I was so thrilled to see J.R.'s bedroom."

What's this popularity mean to the USA? It has had "a generally positive effect" on the USA and its relations with other countries, according to Robert E. Hunter. He's director of European studies at the Center for Strategic and International Studies (CSIS), a Washington-based think tank.

"It means that barriers between countries are coming down. It's more than just an Americanization of the world. It's that people like what's going on in the West. . . . On balance, knowledge about other people is a positive development. The more you know another person, the less likely you are to consider yourself deceived," says Walter R. Roberts, diplomat-in-residence at George Washington University in Washington, D.C.

Interpretation: People get along better when they have something in common. Or to put it another way, China seems a lot closer to the USA when you get on an elevator in Beijing and hear "Love Me Tender" being piped in.

Michael Jackson's 1987–88 "Bad" tour made it clear just how much young people around the world have in common.

In England, they call him "the Earl of Whirl." To Australians, he is "Crocodile Jackson." They adore him in Japan as "Typhoon Michael," while Europeans hail him as the "Pied Piper of Pop."

Whatever the nickname, Jackson epitomizes the worldwide

supremacy, popularity, and unifying nature of USA pop music—
if not USA pop culture in general. Think about it:

• Three million people attended Jackson's tumultuous,
pandemonium-filled concerts.

• In Japan, the tour was the most successful ever by an
international artist—fourteen sold-out shows to 450,000 people.

• He played to 1.4 million people in Europe, including
seven Wembley Stadium concerts in London. Each jam-packed
with 72,000 screaming fans.

"I'm really flabbergasted. I never thought I'd really experience anything like this," said Frank Dileo, Jackson's personal
manager for the "Bad" tour.

Jackson is not only "Bad" in Italy. He's also big.

Since World War II, Italy has been "invaded" by the USA
many times. First it was the GIs. Then the Marshall Plan. Then
jazz and rock 'n' roll. More recently McDonald's. And in the
spring of 1988, Michael Jackson.

He chose Italy to begin the European leg of his tour. And a
visitor to Rome would have had to be blind or deaf to miss the
fact that Michael Jackson was about to enter the old imperial
capital. Banners put up all over the city proclaimed: THE MAGIC
CONTINUES ON TOUR. And it was in English. The language of
global pop culture.

Jackson's hotel in central Rome was constantly mobbed.
He needed a police escort to move about. And even Italian
movie stars such as Sophia Loren and Gina Lollobrigida wanted
to be seen with Jackson when he showed up at the U.S.
Embassy on Rome's famous Via Veneto.

In West Germany, signs all over proclaimed in anglicized
German: DAS ROCK & RAIL HAPPENING 1988. Germany's state-run
federal railroad, Deutsche Bundesbahn, offered Michael Jack-
son fans a special treat: seven extra trains scheduled for four
Jackson concerts in four German cities between July 1 and
July 10.

RIDE THE RAILS AND SEE MICHAEL JACKSON, was the subtitle of
the same six-page, yellow-and-red pamphlets and posters visible at all major railroad stations.

"Aboard the special trains," the announcement stated, "disk jockeys will see to it that Michael Jackson fans arrive at the concerts in the proper mood."

China was on Jackson's itinerary, too. That's where Jet-Capade talked with Guo Dong, twenty, a sophomore majoring in Russian language at Beijing University. Early in the conversation, he made it clear: Rock 'n' roll is a hit in China. One of his favorite rock stars? You guessed it. Michael Jackson.

While Beijing University students sit around the "lake with no name" during a thirty-minute morning break, rock 'n' roll blares from loudspeakers to help them get rejuvenated for the next few hours of classes.

Does this mean that because people from Bonn to Bombay listen to rock 'n' roll and eat hamburgers they also love the USA? No. Of course not. It's easy to find people who are puzzled by U.S. policies. Mystified by the U.S. military. Confused by the U.S. Congress.

And certainly not everybody is a fan of USA popular culture. Take Greek film director Michael Cacoyannis, sixty-five. He brought *Zorba* to the silver screen. "We are subject to a lot of influences from the worst fruits of Western civilization, and that doesn't exclude America," he told us. "I mean like the jukeboxes, video films, bad TV series, blue jeans, and punk haircuts."

But—good or bad, right or wrong—the fact that you can travel to most of the countries in the world and hear the same music and eat the same food and drink the same soft drinks is indisputable.

Perhaps Robert Deutsch, thirty-seven, who owns an antique shop in Old Jaffa, Israel, put it best:

"I deal in the Iron Age, in the Stone Age. But history will look back on this as the American age."

### Rocking 'n' Rolling in Europe

The Oldies But Goodies Record Shop on Paris' narrow Rue du Bourg sells nothing but U.S. music:

• Jazz recordings made in the 1920s through 1940s

• Blues and rock 'n' roll recorded in the 1950s and 1960s

• Country music from the 1980s

"People are starved for good music, and they find it here," said store co-owner Roger Veinante, forty-nine, who had just returned from yet another musical hunt in Texas and Louisiana.

"Jazz, country, and rock from the fifties and sixties are beginning to take off again in the French market. But this is something that isn't only happening in France; it's also in Belgium and Britain," said Veinante's partner, Alain Eginard, forty-two.

Veinante added: "Because the current popular music is generally inferior to that of the forties, fifties, and sixties, many young people here are starved for good music, so they are picking up on everything from John Lee Hooker to B.B. King to country music—anything that's from the United States."

Not too far away, on Rue de L'Abre, another Paris back street, is USA Records—also rolling in oldies.

"Country, rock 'n' roll, rhythm & blues were all born in the U.S.," store owner Daniel Delorme told us. "But they have found a home in France."

Hottest singer at USA Records? Elvis Presley.

The most-requested album: A 1956 recording by rockabilly singer Johnny Burnette with a trio called Burnette's Rock and Roll Trio. Delorme has reordered the album each year since he sold his copy of the original recording for $800 twelve years ago.

"The French have always admired American music," he told us.

In the late 1970s, when punk rock and disco had the

prophets of doom predicting the demise of classic rock 'n' roll, Delorme decided his time had come. He turned a twenty-five-year record-collecting passion into a business.

In 1977, with $130 in his pocket and a personal collection of six thousand records as stock, Delorme opened the doors of USA Records. Today, the shop grosses about $37,000 a month. And more than thirty thousand oldies, original album covers, and record sleeves—as well as six hundred music videos—line the walls of his store. Prices: From $50 to $1,000.

Elvis is also hot 275 miles away at American Sounds, a store specializing in U.S. music on one of Bern, Switzerland's medieval-style streets. The business card tells the story at the Bern store. It's a reproduction of the U.S. flag.

"Elvis Presley is still the favorite," said store co-owner, Dora Cosandey, thirty-seven. "But our biggest seller is country music, which is very popular in Switzerland right now. There are even some local country bands. But they don't sound like the Americans. It's just not the same."

———

### Gunfight at the Munich Corral

Welcome to No Name City.

Here, Indians and cowboys shoot it out on the dusty street. Country music and mariachi sounds are heard in the saloons and honky tonks. And outlaws like Jim Beam and Sam Bass are among the guests on Boot Hill.

Texas? Arizona?

No. This is Poing, an industrial suburb of Munich.

Indeed, No Name City is a small Western-style town surrounded by factories and a railroad track. All the signs are in English (U.S. English) and your deutsche marks are no good here—you use "Nuggets," which look like purple dollar bills.

"This is like stepping into a Hollywood movie set," said Bethel Buckalew, fifty-nine, a geological engineer from Los

Angeles, who now carves horseheads and arrowheads for souvenirs.

"They really like the Western lore in Germany," Buckalew said.

One of the main attractions in No Name City is a tall Cherokee Indian by the name of Buffalo Child. His real name is Silkirtis Nichols, born in Denver, Colorado, sixty-five years ago. He said he's a Cherokee-Choctaw Indian who left the U.S. Army in 1963 after twenty years of service. Much of that time was spent with the U.S. armed forces in West Germany.

"Do the Germans like Western things? They flip out over it. There are now more than two hundred and fifty cowboy clubs in Germany," Nichols said.

No Name City's Golden Nugget Saloon is one of them. Rough-riding Germans go there to swing to the sounds of a band with a country-rock sound—Made in Germany. And across the dusty street at the Mexican Cantina, mariachi music fills the air while patrons knock the imaginary dust out of their throats with a shot of tequila.

But once you pass back through No Name City's entrance, which looks like the front of a fort in a John Wayne Western, it's Germany again—with lots of rules, D-marks, and traffic jams.

———

*A "Bad" Shop*

———

Hundreds of Michael Jackson fans spend thousands of yen each week in Tokyo.

Where? At the Michael Jackson Shop, the only store in the world authorized by the moonwalking phenom to cash in on his name.

His life-size Plexiglas image posed in that now famous "Bad" stance marks the entrance to the shop, sometimes called Hello Michael.

The fans have a yen for gym bags, sweatshirts, T-shirts,

pants, jackets, belts, socks—almost anything that you could put Jackson's name on. And all of it, except one set of U.S.-made T-shirts, is designed and made in Japan.

And the fans buy and buy and buy. "One girl from Osaka bought more than seventy-thousand yen [$580] worth of stuff, practically one of each item," exclaimed Anna Makino, shop clerk.

———

***"Know When to Fold 'Em . . ."***

———

The band played country music and a bit of rock 'n' roll.

The couples, young and old, did what looked like the Texas two-step. Sort of promenading around the semi-dark dance hall in a circle.

The *whoosh* of beer cans popping open punctuated the beat of Kenny Rogers' "The Gambler."

"Know when to hold 'em, know when to fold 'em . . ."

It was all very boisterous and lively. Just about everybody in town was there. It was the Valentine's Day Dance in the town hall of Stanley (population 1,100), the capital of the Falkland Islands. One of the world's smallest and most remote cities—and more than ten thousand miles southeast of Texas.

Stanley looks like an English village, but the mood, dress, feel, and music at the dance were all USA.

Older men wearing coats and ties danced with women in formal dresses. And jean-clad teen-age boys whirled around with girls who looked like they could have stepped off the set of the *Happy Days* TV show.

"The people here are very keen on country music, especially Kenny Rogers," said Pattrick Watts, forty, station manager of FIBS (Falkland Islands Broadcasting Station). FIBS is the only radio station on the islands.

Watts also is the station news editor and broadcaster, and he plays the rhythm guitar in the local country rock band, a quartet with no name, that was playing that night at the Stanley town hall.

They played everything from Kenny Rogers to John Lennon, from Merle Haggard to Elvis Presley.

It cost $1 to get in. That included the right to vote for Miss Valentine.

Joann Bonner, a pretty blond sixteen-year-old looking like the girl next door in the USA, was chosen Miss Valentine 1988.

"It's been great fun," she told us after a victory dance to the beat of another USA rock hit.

———

***"I Can Tell You Anything About Goofy"***

———

Tokyo banker Keisuke Fujii and his wife Kyoko have been to Disneyland five times in five years. Still plan to go once a year each year. Daughter Ayako, three, now goes with them.

It's only a short drive away. To Anaheim? To Orlando?

Nope. To suburban Tokyo.

Disney's been there five years.

Attracts ten million visitors a year. Ninety percent of them Japanese, like the Fujii family.

"My daughter walks around the house singing the Mickey Mouse song in English. She's got us doing it," said Kyoko, thirty-five. "I can tell you almost anything you ever wanted to know about Goofy."

Japan's Disneyland is patterned after California's Disneyland and Florida's Disney World.

Visitors step into a fantasy world full of blond Cinderellas and blue-eyed Prince Charmings—imported college students from the USA.

"We tried to build the original American Disney park as much as possible," said Disney's Toshiharu Akiba.

Tokyo's Disneyland is 50 percent larger than California's. But it has fewer rides: thirty-six to California's fifty. California's Disney averages twenty million visitors a year.

Still most popular attraction: Mickey Mouse.

Many Japanese say they come to Disneyland to teach their kids English.

"It's a little bit of the USA in Tokyo. Everything here is in English," said housewife Akiyo Otazawa, twenty-eight, with her one-year-old child, Natsuki. Both of them were wearing Mickey Mouse ears.

She whispered shyly: "And here, everyone can feel like a child."

Off she went—baby in tow—to the Magic Kingdom.

### A Common Bond

USA popular culture has become a worldwide culture. A shared experience for people from Bonn to Beijing, from Cairo to Canberra, from São Paolo to Singapore.

It's a fast-changing culture laced together with fast food, fast music and fast fads.

It's a culture of unity, not division.

It's a democratic culture for everyone, not just an elite few.

Will it turn the world into an homogenized, mediocre mass? Of course not. People are different. They will remain different.

But a shared popular culture just might make those differences merely delightful, not destructive.

The beat of rock 'n' roll builds bridges, not barriers.

CHAPTER 2

# The Spirit of Sports
# Is a Passion,
# Not a Pastime

Sports and competition are a way of life in much of the world.
Korean Olympic gymnast Park Si Sook, seventeen, trains every
day, every week to reach her goal: an Olympic gold medal.
Photo: Larry Nylund, USA TODAY

C HAMPAGNE was flowing. People were dancing. Horns were honking.

Hundreds of happy Costa Ricans spilled into the streets. Stayed there all night. Yelling, "Long live Costa Rica! Long live Costa Rica!"

They had waited ninety-two years for this day—since the rebirth of the modern Olympics: Costa Rica had just won its first Olympic medal.

The hero: Sylvia Poll, eighteen, winner of a silver medal in the women's 200-meter freestyle swimming competition at the 1988 Summer Olympics in Seoul.

"All the country went crazy," she told us days after winning the silver.

The result: "People, especially little children, look up to me. I see more and more of them swimming or taking part in a sport. For that, I'm terribly happy."

But before the celebration stopped, Poll was back in the pool for her daily workout.

She's preparing for the 1991 World Championships in Australia.

To Poll—and countless others we met—sports is more than a pastime. It's a passion. A way of life.

That spirit of competition that drives our love for sports is alive and well—even in the poorest, most remote sections of the globe.

We're running, walking, jumping, kicking, swimming, and throwing all over the globe:

- In the mountains and in the metropolis
- In teams and in tribes
- With amazing dedication and sophistication

And we haven't stopped since the first known sport—wrestling—was practiced five thousand years ago.

Just how important is sports and physical exercise?

In 1969, when the one-time African state of Biafra was fighting Nigeria for its independence, a seventy-two-hour truce was called to watch Pele—often called the world's greatest soccer player—compete in nearby Lagos with his Santos, Brazil, team.

Or ask South Korean President Roh Tae Woo.

He wears a small pedometer on his belt to count his steps around the presidential palace. Daily average: four thousand.

Or ask millions of Chinese workers.

They bike to work. They have no choice. That's their main form of transportation. Then they spend up to an hour stretching and exercising at their workplace.

"That's how we stay so young," said Zhang Shuming, fifty-six, of Beijing. She runs a parking lot for over seven hundred—of China's two hundred fifty million—bikes. Her fee: two cents a day.

"If we replaced our bicycles with cars, then we wouldn't get any exercise," said Su Ya Li, twenty-five, a nylon products factory worker in Beijing.

But don't worry, Su said. "We wouldn't get fat. We Chinese are always looking for ways to exercise."

So are millions of others. Australians are another example.

Three million of the country's sixteen million are registered in sporting clubs.

"There's a growing trend of people being more involved in some daily form of physical exercise," said Wendy Highett of the state-run Australia Institute for Sports.

"We're trying to make it clear that sports is for all," she added.

Michelle Bowery, seventeen, Australia's two-time national junior tennis champion, says that's the way it should be: "We believe if you have a healthy body, you have a healthy mind. And then you can do anything."

But sports is more than a way to keep fit. It's a key to national and personal pride, a way out of obscurity and into the limelight.

"Now people notice Costa Rica," Poll said. "They are taking time on a map to see where we are."

You couldn't help but take notice of Ireland.

When we arrived there, it was as if the country had just won its independence.

The Boys in Green—their national soccer team—had just beaten England 1–0 in a 1988 European Football (Soccer) Championship match.

Politicians were lauding the country's newfound fame.

Dubliners were singing in the pubs. Drinks were on the house.

Dee-jays were playing "The Boys in Green," a song by the boys themselves. It shot to No. 1.

And a newspaper headline read: PROUD TO BE IRISH.

Everywhere we went, Irish eyes were smiling.

Thousands of miles away, on the tiny South Pacific island of Pago Pago, American Samoa, Governor A. P. Lutali was more than proud to tell us that his island was sending its first Olympic team ever to the Games.

All five athletes.

We also found that:

• Sports goes beyond political and racial realms: It brings the world together.

Over fourteen thousand athletes from 159 nations—the most ever—competed in the Seoul Summer Olympics.

There, athletes from socialist and capitalist countries ran and swam side by side.

They shared dorms, meals, and medals—without major incidents.

Capitalist host country South Korea even used the goodwill of the Games to sign a landmark trade deal with its old nemesis, China. Welcomed a Soviet diplomat for the first time in eighty years. And opened its first Eastern Bloc diplomatic mission in Hungary. It also extended an invitation for its northern communist neighbor, North Korea, to participate.

It's a fact: Few things move us toward unity more surely than the flame, fame, and flags of the Olympic Games.

It's also not uncommon to find sports teams from one country playing in another—even if their governments disagree politically.

Take Cuba.

A group of ninety Italian and four West German bicyclists competed there in 1988 against their Cuban counterparts.

Or the Soviet Union.

The University of Southern California and the University of Illinois football teams planned to play in Glasnost Bowl I in Moscow on September 2, 1989. A Glasnost Bowl II also is planned.

Canadian hockey player Jeffery Denomme, twenty-three, summed it up best: "Hockey has become one of our diplomatic tools."

• Sports heroes are role models extraordinaire.

In Japan, young baseball fans talk about Babe Ruth as if he were their uncle.

In Rome, young basketball fans proudly wear green jerseys emblazoned with a shamrock and No. 33—for Larry Bird of the Boston Celtics.

"The Boston Celtics did for basketball in the 1980s what the Beatles did for music in the 1960s," said Valerio Bianchini, coach of the Italian basketball team, Scavolini.

"Our dreams as kids are the same: We want to grow up to be superstars in the pros," said Juan Antonio Perez, twenty, of Monterrey, Mexico. He works as a waiter and spends the rest of his day playing soccer.

Many sports heroes, like Poll and Cuban track star Alberto Juantorena, told us they want to use their superstar status to encourage exercise.

Juantorena, Cuba's No. 1 superstar, was a two-time Olympic gold medalist at the 1976 Montreal Games.

Now he's using his spectacular status to his advantage.

He just helped start a "grandparents movement" in Cuba to get them to exercise.

Has he been successful? A recent walk attracted 18,600 grandparents, including one ninety-eight-year-old woman, he said.

And that, he told us, is the most satisfying part of his job.

Our role models also are changing the way we think.

Just listen to Masahiko Sunami, eleven, of Tokyo:

"Many schoolboys admire baseball players more than prime ministers. Baseball players are cool. Like the Yankees and Babe Ruth."

We met Sunami when he was at a Tokyo Dome baseball stadium. He was attending one of the twenty baseball games he goes to each season.

"My mother gives me the money to go. She's as much of a baseball fan as I am," he said.

Sunami was dressed like a walking baseball pennant: twenty-five buttons, baseball bat, cap, and flag. All for his favorite team, the Seibu Lions.

• Sports fans are found on all continents—and in the highest political offices.

"For nineteen years, I've been following the [Montreal] Expos [baseball team]," Canadian Prime Minister Brian Mulroney told us.

His prediction: "I think they'll surprise everybody with a World Series."

• Sports is serious business.

Meet Les Yule, forty-three. He's an electrical inspector in Sydney. A member of the North Steyne Surf Lifesaving Club, one of 160 clubs with a total of twenty-five thousand members that compete in lifeboat rowing races, footraces, and mock rescues.

"We train all year round. In winter, we run for endurance and gradually build up to sprints.

"[The rest of the year] we train seven days a week: rowing four days a week and in the gym three days a week."

And, Yule said, "It's all voluntary. There's no chance of being paid."

Throughout JetCapade, we found runners and rowers out at dawn—in the sun and snow—sweating their way through morning workouts.

Like gymnast Seo Mi Sook, eighteen, of Seoul.

Seo—small, spunky, and snappy—trains for twelve hours a day.

She's even given up many of the pleasures most teen-agers enjoy.

"You can't have a steady boyfriend if you're a gymnast because we train so hard," she told us outside the Seoul Olympic Stadium. "But gymnastics are more important. I'm trying my hardest."

But when we met her, she was settling for carrying the gym bags of Olympic gymnasts.

One day, she promised, her training will pay off and people will be carrying her bags.

Swedish track star Patrik Sjoberg, twenty-three, of Gothenburg epitomized the hard work involved in making an Olympic dream reality.

He had one goal in life: to win the gold medal. And nothing was going to stand in his way.

"We are raised in Sweden to finish school and go to college," Sjoberg told us. "Sports has always been viewed as something one does in one's spare time."

But he thought differently.

His teachers told him he needed more homework and less high jump.

"But my way is different: I believed that if I could excel in high jump, I would be a better person."

It worked. Sjoberg won his gold in the 1988 Summer Olympics. He has no regrets.

In some countries, like Cuba, sports is seen as both a right—and a duty. Youths participate whether they like it or not.

"We want sports to become a habit for Cubans, something they do as routinely as eating and sleeping," said Raul Villanueva, forty-five, vice president of Cuba's state-run Institute for Sports and Recreational Activities.

Under Cuban President Fidel Castro, there are now over nine thousand sports sites in Cuba.

Before Castro's 1959 revolution, there were two thousand.

Havana's main Olympic training center is the most modern complex we saw in that city.

It's home to dozens of top Cuban athletes, like little Lourdes Medina.

This small—but strong—twenty-year-old is Cuba's rhythmic gymnastics champ.

And like the other athletes we met around the world, her life revolves around her sport.

"We train six to seven hours a day, except the day we go to classes for four to five hours," Medina said.

"Our best gift to our commander-in-chief is to win our competitions. We want to give him that happiness."

The seriousness of sports competition took a new turn during the Seoul Olympics when it was discovered that sprinter Ben Johnson of Canada had evidence of steroids in his blood.

Johnson, who was forced to return his medal, became the center of the controversy: How seriously do we take sports and exercise?

In the U.S.S.R., East Germany, China, Cuba, and other socialist countries, the answer is: Very serious, with a capital *V.*

Soviet athletes who win gold medals can be paid up to $19,000, according to Marat Gramov, head of the Soviet Olympic Committee.

Cuban athletes wear or use equipment with the initials LPV—*Listos Para Vencer,* Spanish for "Prepared for Victory."

In nearly all communist countries, potential superstars are moved at an early age into sports camps, where they are educated and trained.

Listen to Vladimir Veremeyev, forty, former Soviet soccer player and now manager of the U.S.S.R.'s Dynamo Kiev soccer team: "Soviet athletes do well internationally because the communist party and officials take a lot of care about sports. They take sports seriously because sports is the ambassador of peace.

"Dynamo does well [in soccer] by sending coaches all over the Ukraine looking for talented players. We run a special football school for promising young athletes. We start keeping files on prospective players when they are as young as eight years old," he said.

The Soviets—like the USA and other countries—even have sports down to a science.

The Moscow Research Institute of Physical Culture predicts how many Olympic medals the USA, East Germany, and the Soviet Union will win each Olympics. It claims a 90 percent accuracy rate.

• Sports is big business.

A sampling of sports salaries:

Magic Johnson, basketball, USA, $2.5 million annually.

Ivan Lendl, tennis, Czechoslovakia, $2.4 million annually.

Ian Woosnam, golf, Wales, $1.8 million.

High salaries for high rollers.

They attract large crowds—and excite them with their magic.

But big bucks also can be made in product endorsements.

Just look at the top tennis players at Wimbledon decked out in shirts advertising major product lines.

The money is not only made on the field but off, too.

The 1992 Olympics in Barcelona is expected to generate $2.6 billion in tourist income.

Finally, sporting events around the world generate the biggest excitement—and TV ratings.

The world comes to a near standstill for the final game of the World Cup soccer tournament, held every four years.

Two billion people tuned in in 1986 for the final match held in Mexico City. Many more are expected to tune in for the finals in Rome in 1990.

Or the Olympic gold medal competition in figure skating, basketball, or gymnastics.

Three billion people—the most ever—watched the Seoul Olympics.

Another 3.5 billion are expected to watch the 1992 Barcelona Summer Olympics.

Clearly, the more we traveled on JetCapade, the more we found people walking, running, and exercising—for fun, for health, for competition.

Said Swedish track star Patrik Sjoberg:

"We have a lot of healthy people here in Sweden because of simple things, like taking a walk in the forest.

"It gives us pleasure. And we do those things because they make us feel better."

Added Australian tennis star Bowery: "There's nothing more I'd rather do than play tennis. Sports is a passion for me. Isn't it for everyone?"

———

### Don't Kill the Umpire, Bow to Him

———

*Shhhh.* You're at a Japanese baseball game.

That's right.

No loud screaming. No hysterical fans.

Just a stadium full of polite, respectful, and often quiet people.

You'd never guess it, but Japan "is baseball crazy," said Wayne Graczyk, author of the annual *Japan Pro Baseball Fan Handbook.*

But the Japanese have put their own spin on the game:

Players bow to umpires.

Fans return foul balls.

Noodles and sake instead of hotdogs and beer.

"Baseball is our soccer," said Japanese businessman Takuya Ichikawa, twenty-two, at the Tokyo Dome, where many baseball games are played. "But we don't jump up and scream as much as the people of the USA. It's our national characteristic not to get excited."

Even the game strategy is conservative, according to Graczyk. "They have a saying here that the nail that sticks up gets hammered down. So all the managers are alike."

Examples: "If the lead-off man gets on base, they bunt. If the lead-off man in the first inning gets a triple, they play the infield run, even in the first inning. In the [U.S.] major leagues, you don't do that till the ninth inning," says Graczyk.

Japanese fans can be divided into two camps: those who like the Yomiuri Giants and those who don't.

The Giants are the oldest and winningest team in Japan and command 70 percent of the fans.

But there's an Association of Anti-Giants People.

The rivalry can be intense—Japanese-style.

Sometimes the fans get so excited they do stand up and scream—but only for a second.

Those are the ones in the cheap seats.

"The people in the box seats pay forty dollars a game and they don't move. The real baseball fans are up there," Ichikawa said, pointing to the bleachers.

"They pay six-fifty, so they can afford to come to all the games. They can get very excited," he said.

And where does Ichikawa sit?

Sometimes in the box seats.

Sometimes in the cheap seats, "When I need to stand up and clap to the music. I have to let out my excitement somehow."

**U.S. Football Fever Strikes in Germany**

For centuries, soccer—called football everywhere except in the USA—has been king in Europe.

Now there's a newcomer on the block—one that's running away with German loyalty. It's also called football. Only it's the U.S. style.

At the forefront of popularity: Adler, the 1987 German Super Bowl Champs. One of 120 amateur teams in West Germany.

It's been difficult for German fans—and players, most of whom have never played U.S. football—to understand the game. But once they do, they get the same fever that grips millions in the USA.

"I thought rugby and football were the same until I saw the Adler play," said Frank Stahnke, nineteen, an Adler wide receiver.

"Football is more impressive to me. It's more organized, like the military. Rugby looks stupid beside it."

A newspaper poll conducted at the end of the Adler's season last year found them to be more popular than the local Berlin ice hockey and soccer teams.

"That really made the soccer mafia mad," said team spokesperson Barbara Brockhoff. "We hope they'll learn to live with it."

The team averages three thousand fans a game but had seventeen thousand for its final game last year.

The players get no salary. Most hold full-time jobs. Local sporting goods stores donate equipment. Berlin city officials pay for thirty-five of the team's forty-five players to fly to games throughout Germany.

The Adler's coach is from the USA: Billy Brooks, a former wide receiver with the Cincinnati Bengals and Houston Oilers.

To keep the game fair, only two players from the USA are allowed on the field at one time for each team.

"We want American football to be a top sport for Germans," Brockhoff said. "But right now, American players have the expertise."

But Berlin isn't the only place fascinated by football.

• Over forty-four thousand fans attended a Boston College vs. U.S. Army football game in November 1988—in Dublin, Ireland.

• Over thirty-three thousand attended a Minnesota Vikings vs. Chicago Bears game in August 1988 in Gothenburg, Sweden.

• And football games are planned in the Soviet Union.

For now, most foreign football games are played by college rules—four 15-minute quarters.

But that's not where the similarities end.

Just ask Stahnke.

When we interviewed him he was on the bench—with an injured hand.

"A player needs heart to play American football. It's a tough game."

———

### "I'm Trying to Make Tennis My Life"

———

Sports runs in this family.

So much so that they're known as Australia's First Family of Tennis.

There's the mother, Lesley Turner, forty-eight.

Winner of the 1962 and 1964 Wimbledon mixed doubles championships, the 1964 Wimbledon doubles championship and the 1963 and 1965 French Open tournaments.

There's the father, Bill Bowery, forty-three.

He played on Australia's Davis Cup Team in 1968 and 1969. Now a tennis pro at the Sydney's White City Tennis Club and a TV tennis commentator.

And then there's the daughter, Michelle Bowery, seventeen.

"Ugh. I'm sick of being asked about my parents."

"People are always saying 'She's Lesley's daughter or Bill's daughter.' I want it to be reversed," said the feisty—but feminine—Michelle.

That could happen one day.

Michelle is a two-time national junior tennis champ and is about to join the international tennis circuit.

She's considered one of Australia's brightest young prospects.

When we met her, she was about to begin her after-school workout at White City Tennis Club—in the rain.

"My friends don't understand why I don't party with them or go to the beach. I'm trying to make tennis my life and my job."

Her parents work out with her daily—something she knows gives her an added edge.

"They're pretty critical and get upset at me. And I get upset at them. But it's worth it. I dream of holding the French Open trophy. Mom did that twice, you know."

It doesn't take much to see that this woman is intent on being the best.

"I don't think about losing. Australians don't, either. We're a very competitive country."

Of course, there's a price to pay for everything. And being a woman tennis star is no exception.

"Guys don't ask me to play tennis anymore. Guys don't like losing to girls. It hurts their egos," she said. "I lost a friendship for a few days because I beat a guy six-love."

She then squealed and added:

"But I enjoyed that."

### Basketball Has Full-Court Press on World

Football may be tackling Germany, but basketball is the USA's top sports export.

It's hot. Very hot.

Example: The National Basketball Association (NBA) is now seen on TV in seventy-six countries.

"Right now, we're the world's most widely distributed sports property, with the exception of the Olympics," said Ed Desser, vice president/general manager of the NBA International.

"We pretty much have the world covered," Desser said. "The only continent we're missing is Antarctica."

NBA hot spots: Italy, Spain, and Yugoslavia.

There, NBA telecasts are a weekly event.

Why is it so popular?

"Basketball has been in the Olympics for years. It's a sport which quite a few countries play. A lot of people have an understanding for the game," Desser said.

Besides watching televised games, Europeans are attending live ones. In Italy, former USA basketball stars are a key draw. Among the many: Bob McAdoo, Artis Gilmore, and Greg Ballard.

In downtown Madrid, Spain, there's even a store specializing in NBA gear, appropriately called Viva Basketball.

### Hong Kong's Horse Racing Is Unbridled

The spirit of competition is at a full gallop at Hong Kong's Royal Jockey Club. But the only things staying in shape are the horses and the winners' wallets.

More money is bet at this racetrack than at any other in the world: up to $64.2 million a day.

It has all the modern conveniences, for horse bettors and horses alike.

But many fear it may all come to an end.

Horse racing is seen as a symbol of decadent colonialism in China—set to assume control of Hong Kong in 1997. Thousands of fans fear that's when their luck will run out. But China promises it won't drastically change Hong Kong for at least fifty years.

"People will keep their existing lifestyles," assured Ji Shaoxiang of the Xinhua News Agency—representing China in the transition.

"China will not be foolish," he added.

Still, bettors worry. Especially since the track is fourteen miles south of China's border.

There is hope: All earnings from the nonprofit track go to schools, parks, and other civic ventures.

And with a record take of $64.2 million in one day and daily averages of $6.4 million, horse betting is too much of an institution in Hong Kong to take it away, advocates said.

"I don't know anywhere in the world you'd find a population so committed to betting," said Robin Parke, racing writer for the *South China Morning Post.*

"The [bets] here are by far the highest in the world," she said.

Attendance at each race: an average of fifty thousand.

The facilities are also top-notch.

For the horses:

• An indoor swimming pool
• A fully-equipped hospital
• An all-grass racing track

For the bettors:

• A hundred twenty machines throughout Hong Kong where bettors can shift money from bank accounts into betting accounts
• Machines and video screens to allow for betting on races at other tracks
• Express trains to bring the faithful directly to the track entrance
• An infield park with palm trees, swans, and fountains

• Saunas, squash courts, exercise rooms, a pool and restaurants

As one bettor put it, horse racing at the Royal Jockey Club is horse racing fit for a king.

———

### Nothing Stops Him from Reaching the Top

———

Ulrich Inderbinen, eighty-eight, has a formula for long life:

Live simply.

Be polite to others.

Climb mountains—which is synonymous with "stay in shape."

"I have grown old together with the mountains," said the browned, weathered, and wrinkled mountaineer.

And he knows those spiny ridges like the back of his hand.

Inderbinen is the oldest mountain guide in Zermatt, Switzerland—and perhaps Europe.

His workplace: the breathtaking Swiss Alps.

He grew up in the shadow of the biggest of the Alps: Monte Rosa (15,203 feet) and Matterhorn (14,692 feet).

In Inderbinen's friendly, fatherly way, he guides customers up crackling crevices, around steep slopes, and through shin-deep snow.

It's the only job he knows and wants to do.

The inspiration for his decision: the sharp spire of the majestic Matterhorn jutting into the cottonlike clouds. He studied it each day as he walked to and from school in Zermatt.

"I knew I would make my living, somehow, from that mountain," he reflected.

Inderbinen's step is a little slower these days but still sure. He said he's made only one concession in his advancing years: He stopped tackling the Matterhorn.

Still, thousands try to climb it each year.

Last year, 31 died trying, 3 are still missing, and 136 had to be rescued by helicopter.

Inderbinen replaced the Matterhorn with ski racing. He's usually the only entrant in the eighties-and-older class.

"So I come in first and last," he told us with a laugh.

But all that is like melted snow when it comes to his first love: climbing mountains.

"When you're just a boy, you can be tending your father's cows in a pasture. And you see a flower blowing in the wind above you, very high up in the rock. So, you have to climb up there to get it. And you decide nothing will stop you from reaching that flower. And that, my friend, is when you learn to climb a mountain."

——

**United by Desire to Win**

——

Sports competition is compulsive around the world. We're obsessed with the idea of keeping fit. Of being the best. Of being winners. We worship the superstars. Watch the World Cup.

And even though we're thousands of miles away, we cheer and cry with our Olympians as they get their moment in the satellite spotlight.

But sports is more than that.

It's a plus for national pride and international understanding. Nothing can bring us closer together than sports. The spirit of competition crosses most racial and political boundaries.

Athletes become goodwill ambassadors. The playing field is their forum.

Regardless of what language we speak or customs we practice, we all play the same sports.

We all play by the same rules.

"You're safe!" or "You're out!" is the same in any language.

# CHAPTER 3

# The Past Makes Our Present Special

Hundreds of proudly practiced traditions give countries and their people an identity and a heritage. Pilar Rospide, twenty-two, is a shining example. She's one of Madrid's finest flamenco dancers.

Photo: Callie Shell, *Nashville Tennessean*

A SPANIARD tipped us off: The best flamenco starts after midnight.

That's when La Chunga, Lucia, and Pilar Rospide take the stage.

Or rather, commandeer it.

Pilar, twenty-two—tall, slender, and sensuous—left her audience of Spaniards in Madrid mesmerized.

They clapped as she clicked her *palillos*—wooden shells—and tapped her heels at lightning speed.

Yelled "Olé" and "Viva" as she twisted and twirled her long brown hair and long red ruffled and polka-dotted dress.

Listened quietly and intently as she sang:

I gave you the most wonderful thing I had . . . myself.
But now you act like you don't know me.
Why do you break my heart?

It's a dance "born of the first cry and the first kiss," said Spain's poet laureate Federico García Lorca.

Passed down from generations.

Prized by natives and tourists.

Performed by young and old.

The fabled flamenco: Spanish folklore at its best.

One of hundreds of traditions proudly practiced from Paris to Perth, Palermo to Pago Pago. Each different but all giving their countries an identity, a uniqueness, a heritage. Setting people and places apart. Telling others: "This is my culture. This is my country. We're special. And we're proud."

And that pride for our past seems to be growing.

Three examples from three different parts of the world:

• Australia: People are searching for their roots with a new enthusiasm—and holding their heads high. Even though the ancestors of most Australians were convicts.

Government officials opened up genealogy records in 1974.

Since then, the number of people searching for their roots and traditions has grown steadily to thirty-five hundred in 1987.

"These days, discovering a convict ancestor seems to spur people on," said Margaret Bryant, a Tasmanian archivist. "It's the thrill of the chase."

• China: A chef's school is teaching students how to cook the way their ancestors did—twenty-five hundred years ago.

China's Cultural Revolution belittled the culinary arts as a feudal practice.

Now the ancient art is surging.

Result: Attendance at the Guangzhou (Canton) Chef's School has been building steadily in the last fifteen years.

"We have the duty to carry on the tradition so it won't disappear," said Chef Xu Liqing, thirty-eight. "It's our responsibility."

• Scotland: Bagpipes and kilts—which the English tried to stamp out in the mid-1700s—are prospering.

Also "in": restorations of everything from pyramids and palaces to cities and cemeteries.

In Riyadh, Saudi Arabia, antiquities and museums director Abdullah H. Masry, forty, said, "In the past, people went ahead with merciless zeal to remove old towns. In that rush and that zeal I daresay we lost a few jewels."

But today, those jewels—in many different forms—are being spared, restored, or revived.

Why? So our countries and cultures can keep their identity.

"It's important that Paris doesn't look like Rome or London—but like Paris. And it's even more important that Paris doesn't look like Caracas," said Michel Guy, head of Paris' Festival d'Automne, an annual arts festival.

People of all ages are concluding: Our past makes our present special.

Listen to Anne Marie Caulfield, twenty, a Dublin secretary: "In rural Ireland, most of the young people keep the many Irish traditions. If you don't, you're considered an outsider."

Many of the people we met told us traditions "are written in the blood"—they are either inherited or instinctive.

Italian gondolier Umberto Pavan, sixty, of Venice: "My father, my grandfather were gondoliers. The city gives you a license. It gets passed down from father to son."

Spanish bullfighter Rafael Camino, nineteen, of Madrid: "No one can ever teach you how to fight a bull. My father [bullfighter Paco Camino] couldn't teach me. It comes from inside you."

Then there's the 748-year-old tradition in Krakow, Poland, that causes many to stop in their tracks. They watch. Listen. And remember.

Every hour on the hour.

Twenty-four hours a day.

Three hundred and sixty-five days a year. (That is, if the wind holds out.)

There, trumpeters blow their horns atop St. Mary's Church like one of their ancestors did in 1241.

He was warning people of the invasion of the Tatars—a people set on taking over Eastern Europe.

That trumpeter was silenced by an arrow through the neck.

Today the trumpet-playing continues, to remind the people of their heritage. This time by members of the Professional Fire Brigade.

"These are not concert hall conditions—especially when the wind blows. But we realize this is an honor," said trumpeter Tadeusz Kaczmarczyk, forty-two.

We found people couldn't talk about tradition and culture without talking about how they feel toward their country.

Take Mexican piñata maker Teresa Jimenez, fifty-five, of Saltillo, Mexico.

"One man offered to move me to America, give me a house, and make sure my children got an education if I would go help start a piñata business in Los Angeles," she said.

It was an easy decision.

"Piñatas are a tradition here," she told him. "I don't want to leave my home."

Then there's Eduardo Islas Perea.

Like most people, his pride is not only in his country, but in his craft.

"I put my special touch into my piñatas—I put more effort into my work than most people do," explained Islas, fifty-seven, a Tijuana piñata maker.

"If people tell me how to make them, I say, 'Take your business elsewhere. This is my craft.' I put my time into my work and don't rush when I make a Mexican piñata."

Sometimes the traditional ways of doing things conflict with the modern way of doing things.

Case in point: pop culture.

It's spreading around the globe via TV, movies, and music videos.

"The TV network is the real ministry of culture here," said Vassilis Vassilikos, fifty-four, of Athens, Greece—author of the famous 1966 novel *Z*.

That culture often includes:
- Fast food
- Blue jeans
- Rock 'n' roll music

But people are fighting back.

"If I can get just one teen-age couple to give up rock 'n' roll music and carry on the tradition of the tango, I will have accomplished something," declared Juan Carlos Copes, fifty-six, of Buenos Aires.

He's considered Argentina's best tango dancer.

"The tango is Argentina," he said. "Other countries may have made it more popular or publicized it more, but we did it first. The tango is Argentina's dance."

The problem has come to a head in India.

There, arranged marriages are big, albeit illegal.

Dowries were outlawed in 1962 but fathers of prospective brides are still expected to deliver "purity"—and pay the groom's family handsomely.

Often parents pick their child's mate without the advice of their son or daughter.

Just look in the *Sunday Times* of India.

You'll see nearly two pages of classified ads with the headings GROOMS WANTED and BRIDES WANTED.

The problems of prearranged romance sent two young law students in New Delhi into the park—to hide from their parents.

We met Suresh Kait, twenty-five, and Saroj Bala, twenty-four, at the Sanjay Gandhi Park.

They're engaged but their parents don't plan on the wedding until 1990.

"Our parents didn't know we had fallen in love before they arranged the engagement," Kait said. "Nobody likes these old customs, but we must accept them."

Added Bala, striking in her red native costume: "Today, I said I was going to see a friend who had an accident. Instead I came here to the park to meet Suresh. We can talk and kiss here. It's exciting to do it this way."

As for the future: "When we have our kids, they will not have to listen," Kait said. "They will be free to date whomever they choose."

Efforts to revive a forgotten tradition can often bring its own unexpected problems.

Just ask Mary O'Rourke, thirty, of Dublin, Ireland.

She spins her own wool and designs and weaves rugs and sweaters.

"Older people come up to me horrified that I still spin my own wool. They associate that with poverty and hard times," O'Rourke told us.

"In their day, families kept two or three sheep to clothe twelve kids. Spinning wool was considered a chore."

But rest assured, Mary O'Rourke will go on spinning.

And so will the tradition.

—

### Potpourri of Palates Provides Flavor

—

Snake bile.

Eel soup.

Fried young pigeon.

Crab claws adorned by a hundred flowers.

Antelope, giraffe, and wild boar meat.

Common cuisines for the world's people.

Exotic delights for world travelers.

What's served—and how it's prepared and eaten—is as much a tradition in some countries as is baseball, apple pie, and Chevrolet in the USA.

Food expresses culture, history, and art.

It *is* culture, history, and art, advocates say.

Take France. Nowhere is food taken more seriously.

"Here one goes to the big restaurants like one goes to the opera," said Raymond Armisen, president of the Fondation Auguste Escoffier, a culinary school and museum in Villeneuve-Loubet, France.

In France, a good chef is a celebrity. A great one is a hero. And Auguste Escoffier? He's close to canonization.

"Thanks to him, cooking is an art," Armisen said.

Escoffier was the chef at the Savoy and Carlton hotels in London and at the Ritz in Paris. He authored the *Guide Culinaire*—a chef's Bible—and created the dessert called peach melba.

Chefs invoke his name like that of a saint. He's credited with giving France its worldwide reputation for good taste.

Just how serious is food and the culinary arts in France? Ask those following in the legacy of Escoffier.

"The pleasures of preparing a table are a tradition in France," explained Christian Guillut, thirty-three, chief chef at the Ritz cooking school in Paris.

Waiting tables "is more than a job. It's a profession," said Robert Grattepanche, thirty-eight, maître d'hôtel at the Jules Verne Restaurant atop the Eiffel Tower.

And "whenever more than three Frenchmen are together, they will discuss food at one time or another," Guillut added.

The French are so proud of their expertise in food that they go so far as to say they are born with it.

Or, as Armisen put it: "The French have a more sensitive palate."

But if cooking is an art in France, it's a delicacy in China.

The Chinese pride themselves on being able to cook almost everything: rats, cats, jellyfish, sea slugs, and land snakes.

Dishes like thousand-year-old eggs and snake bile are traditional treats.

Once served exclusively to the emperors, many are now served to the "people." Meals can include dozens of courses before often concluding with soup.

In Guangzhou, China's Snake Restaurant, waiters bring a wire basket with a dozen slithering snakes—some of them poisonous—to your small table.

Patrons around you stop to watch what's about to happen.

The waiter carefully picks out a three-foot-long snake, which appears to be a brown cobra. His right hand holds the snake behind its neck. His left hand holds its tail.

The snake fights to break loose. But the waiter holds on. Brings the fighting snake close for your inspection.

You nod.

He puts the snake down on the restaurant floor. His right foot behind its head. His left hand on its tail. The snake continues fighting.

He then slowly slides his hand down the snake's slick skin. Finds what he's looking for.

Makes a small incision into its skin with a small sharp pocket knife. Pop. Out comes the gallbladder.

The snake squirms to break free. It's quickly put into the basket. Taken away to be killed.

The waiter picks up the gallbladder. Mashes it in a bowl. Pours the green bile into a clear liquid. Puts it on the table.

Served as a drink.

A Chinese delicacy.

What does it taste like? Bile, said JetCapade editor/reporter John M. Simpson.

A traditional treat that neither memory nor stomach will soon forget.

———

### *"Our Children Should Stay Here"*

———

They are people of the past who are fearful of the future. All they ask is that they be left alone.

But that isn't happening.

This is Kenya's Masai tribe: traditional warriors and sheep herders known for their skillful use of weapons and their strong independent ways.

The Masai live in igloolike huts made of mud, cow dung, and branches. Have no electricity, refrigeration, or stoves. Clad themselves in colorful one-piece cloths. Dot the red clay foothills of Kenya's countryside.

As part of his manhood, a Masai warrior—called a *moran*—must kill a lion with a spear and adorn himself with red-ochered locks.

But no more.

The Kenyan government has outlawed both in the latest attempt to bring the Masai into the twentieth century.

And that's what has them worried.

"We are no longer doing ceremonies for the *moran*," said

Charles Loiboni, twenty, a member of the last class of the *moran.* "That is over."

But he argues: "This is where our children should stay."

Others seem to agree.

Recent newspaper reports say Masai who give up herding and move to the city are risking high blood pressure and heart disease.

Observers say Masai—stripped of their traditional roles and offered nothing in contemporary society to replace it—are becoming alcoholics.

But for Loiboni, the transition into modern society has already begun.

He wears Western clothing, commutes to work as a clerk at a roadside refreshment stand, and speaks English learned at his mission school.

For a fee, he escorts visitors into his village of Olorgasaille (population 50) and provides translation.

It's also where we met *moran* Mula Leoyie.

He had his staff in hand, was draped in a sheet of red-and-plaid fabric, and was adorned with traditional bracelets and earrings.

He does not speak English and has never been to Nairobi, fifty miles away.

Except for the occasional visitors, Leoyie and the other Masai live largely secluded.

And want it that way.

"This is where our children should stay because they were born here," said Noomatasian Loiboni, sixty-five, the village's eldest woman and Charles' grandmother. "But I fear when they are sixteen or older, they will move to Nairobi or some other part of the world."

And if they do, the Masai say that will be the end of their traditional tribe.

**"You Have to Have Diver's Blood"**

It's 136 feet to the bottom. Straight down. At lightning speed.

And when you walk out to the edge of the rock, there's no turning back—no matter how scared you are.

"The fear, it doesn't leave you," said Rolando Carbajal, twenty-four, an Acapulco cliff diver. "You just have to dominate it."

He does. Several times a day. After praying to the Lady of Guadalupe for protection.

He's one of Acapulco's thirty-six cliff divers—famous the world over for their death-defying dives.

Their acts are admired by the tourists.

Adored by young women.

Despised by their mothers.

"She tells me I'm crazy," said Roberio Pelaez, twenty-seven, of Acapulco—a nine-year veteran. So crazy, he said, that she won't watch him dive.

Pelaez's fellow divers have broken their arms, ribs, and other body parts when they hit the water.

The key: Hitting the wave when it's the fullest. Then the water will be twelve feet deep. If they miss, it's only a few feet deep.

"There are times when it's very windy. When the ocean's very rough. When the public throws garbage out . . . a flash cube, a bottle which you don't see. That's when there are accidents," said diver Monico Ramirez, thirty.

The tradition started when fisherman would dive to free their anchors from the rocks. It then became a way to prove valor or impress women.

Today the fishermen—many of whom still dive to free their nets—gather in their boats around the rocks to watch their protégés perform. The daily cliff-diving tradition has become synonymous with Acapulco.

"My father was a diver. The majority of my family were divers. You have to have diver's blood," Carbajal said.

Today, when a diver becomes good enough, he can apply for membership into a union and earn about $50 a week. Most have other jobs.

But is it worth it?

"I stand up there sometimes and want to stay on the rock. I don't want to dive. I sweat. I get anxious," Pelaez said.

Sometimes, he told us, he thinks, "There's got to be an easier way to make a living."

———

**Acupuncture Balances Yin and Yang**

———

Just the thought of it hurts.

Three-inch-long needles being pushed into the skin.

To relieve pain?

It works, insists Qu Zhengliang, thirty-one, a Beijing, China, acupuncturist.

So well, in fact, that she treats "all kinds of pain."

The secret: Something called the yin and yang.

According to Chinese philosophy, disease and pain occur because of an imbalance between the yin and yang—two forces of nature. Acupuncture restores this balance.

"In Western medicine, they just discuss nerve systems. But traditional Chinese medicine also considers there is a potential nerve system which cannot be seen by the eye. I want to preserve that," Zhengliang said.

Doctors have even used acupuncture to relieve pain during major surgery since the 1950s. Its popularity is spreading.

"Many countries are paying attention to traditional Chinese medicine now and are using it alongside modern medicine," Zhengliang maintained.

Where acupuncture is done on the body doesn't depend on the location of the pain.

Example: "For a headache, the needle doesn't go on the head but on the foot. If the pain is on the right, the needle goes on the left side.

"Acupuncture is a question of points on the body—major points and supporting points," Zhengliang explained.

Zhengliang then looked at us and read our minds—and our stomachs.

"For nausea," she said, "it's a point on the wrist and a point on the leg."

We passed.

### *"We Believe in Chocolate"*

Hans-Joerg Meier is keeping a Swiss tradition alive—chocolate-making.

"We've been chocolate innovators and producers for more than a hundred and forty years," Meier said. He's president of Lindt-Spruengli, Switzerland's third-largest chocolate manufacturer and its No. 1 exporter.

"Chocolate is for us a tradition," Meier said during an interview at his firm's headquarters on the shores of Lake Zurich, the smell of chocolate filling the air. "We believe in chocolate, and we think in chocolate terms. Chocolate is, if you will, most of our life."

Mouth-watering Swiss brand names like Suchard, Tobler, Nestlé, and of course Spruengli and Lindt are those of actual nineteenth century Swiss who pioneered the country's chocolate industry.

No matter where you go in Switzerland, there's chocolate:
- Dark chocolate, white chocolate, milk chocolate
- Chocolate balls, bars, squares, and cones
- Liquor-filled chocolates, chocolates with nuts, chocolate truffles, and chocolate drinks

"It's a product that gives pleasure, and we want to give people pleasure," Meier said.

***The Samba Is
in Their Blood***

Rio de Janeiro shakes and shimmies with the samba. The dance is more of a religion there than a form of recreation.

One evening at the Mangueira Schola de Samba will make you a believer. Total members: ten thousand. One of Rio's biggest.

The dancers packing the floor are some of the same ones who pack Rio streets for five days and nights dancing, drinking, and parading during Carnival—the annual pre-Lenten celebration.

One of the dancers was Maria Fatima LaBoto. She proudly displayed her laminated club card and proclaimed:

"I have Mangueira in my blood. It's part of our culture. It's part of our nation. Mangueira preserves our culture."

The Mangueira school, like many others, is in the heart of a *favela,* a section of shantytowns that has grown up in Rio's hills. The schools often are the center of these communities.

"The school is family. It's home. It's everything," said Otacillo, forty-four, a samba composer. (Brazilians often use only a first name or nickname.)

The Cariocas, as the people of Rio call themselves, prepare all year for the grand finale: the samba parade in the Carnival.

"We rehearse. We train. We practice. We wait," Andreia Gama, seventeen, told us.

Why?

"The biggest emotion of every sambista is that they get to go in the samba parade," Otacillo said.

### Bullfighting Takes Style

Rafael Camino considers himself an artist—not a sportsman.

His canvas: a bullring.

His brush: a cape and sword.

His paint: a ferocious bull.

"This is an art but you have to prepare for it like an athlete," said Camino, nineteen, one of Spain's up-and-coming bullfighters.

"It's not a fight of who's going to win. The people are watching my style."

And the bull. All one thousand pounds of it. Snorting. Panting. Ready to charge. Ready to kill.

But the bull has very little chance to win this—or any other—fight.

He will die—much to the delight of the Spaniards. It's tradition.

But now people are banding together—again—to try to change that.

The Spanish Animal Rights Association and several European Parliament deputies have launched a European petition drive to ban bullfighting in Spain and France and fox hunting in Britain, France, and Ireland.

Organizers want animal protection legislation passed in all twelve European Community countries.

They are not alone in their dislike for the art.

Many Spaniards call it cruel. Tourists—who cheer for the bull—often leave disgusted after the first of three bullfights per afternoon.

But these opponents—like many others who have tried in the past and failed—have an uphill battle.

Bullfighting is Spain's best-known sport and biggest spectator sport. And art.

The cultural life of Spanish villages often revolves around the bullfight.

Leading matadors like Camino—son of one of Spain's most famous bullfighters, Paco Camino—are national heroes.

Bullfighting's popularity continues to grow.

• Twenty-three million people attended bullfights in 1988, three million more than in 1987.

• There were 566 "major" bullfights in 1988, 11 percent more than in 1987 and the highest number this decade.

• Forty-nine of Spain's fifty provinces have permanent bull-rings.

• Thousands of temporary rings are set up in towns and villages during the summer months.

"People get scared because of the blood. They think the animal is suffering, but the animal is nervous and doesn't realize what he's doing," Camino said.

"They will never outlaw bullfighting, no matter how much people are against it. People will never let that happen. If they do, it will be crazy. You will lose Spain's culture."

———

***Tradition Sets Us Apart***

———

Other traditions living on with dignity:

• Mexico: Mariachis—in black suits and sombreros—serenade with guitars, trumpets, and violins. For young Latin lovers and rich-tipping tourists.

• Argentina: Gauchos—ranchers—tend cattle and farm fields in rugged cowboy leather.

• Cuba: Cigar-making, tobacco-twisting traditionalists roll their products by hand, one by one.

• Egypt: Papyrus—the world's first paper, now touted as the only true paper—flourishes in artwork.

• Saudi Arabia: Egyptian architects restore clay and stone ruins in the land of the new and plenty.

• Australia: Aborigine art—once forgotten—in museums. A new source of pride for beleaguered tribes.

• Japan: Geisha girls—once big in number—still practice age-old serving customs to a rich, celebrated few.

• Greece: Plate-breaking to release frustrations and laud fine dancers is still big—if breakers agree to pay for plates.

• Spain: The country proudly prepares for 1992 and the five hundredth anniversary of the European discovery of America by Columbus—a pioneer time has not forgotten.

• Italy: Generations of gondoliers row through Venice canals. Making money and memories.

• Ireland: Leprechauns are gone; but literary heroes, folk music, and the once-dying Celtic language are here to stay.

• England: Shakespearean actors recreate timeless plays to packed appreciative audiences.

• Canada: The French are standing strong to preserve their lifestyle and language in Quebec.

Our traditions and culture not only set us apart but are part of our very being.

They shaped the lives of our ancestors, are now shaping our lives, and will shape the lives of those who follow us.

It's our past that makes our present special. Makes us proud to say, "These are my people. This is my country."

# CHAPTER 4

# We Love the Country We Call Home

Country pride takes all shapes and forms. At the 1988 Calgary Winter Olympics, Canadians and Americans celebrated their countries' victories all night long.

Photo: © Elliott Erwitt/Magnum Photos

ROSALINDA Magana, twenty, of Michoacán, Mexico, lined up outside the U.S. Embassy in Mexico City. At 5:30 A.M. She was one of hundreds.

She was there for a visa. To pick fruit and vegetables in the USA. To earn money. For herself. Her family. She'll work over twelve hours a day.

And though lured by the prosperity of the USA, she said she'll return each night to sleep in her beloved Mexico. As she has for the past several years. Mexico, she said, is her home. It's where her heart is. Where she belongs.

"I've been in the United States many times. It's a nice place to work, but I don't want to live up there," Magana said. "Mexico is my country. I'm going to make it work for me."

She's not alone. Millions feel the same way. Call it pride. Call it patriotism.

It's a feeling we found everywhere. In Mexico and Manila. Moscow and Madrid. In every corner and crevice of the globe. No matter how poor, how rich the people, their land, or their heritage.

And it's as strong as ever.

Listen to two well-traveled experts:

• "Nationalism and love of country remain one of the most powerful forces operating in the world today—especially in the developing areas," said Long Island University President David Steinberg, who has studied nationalism. "It's an ideology that gives cohesion and defines a common identity, a sense of collective self."

• "I see it everywhere—even in countries that don't have much of anything—and there are no signs of it diminishing," said James T. Hackett, a former career diplomat and now international affairs expert at the Heritage Foundation, a Washington-based think tank. "Even the Soviet Union—the last great empire—is beginning to break up as the different nationalities become more conscious of their own identities."

We may criticize our homeland. Even leave it. But we hold a special place for it in our heart. It's something nearly all of us have in common.

Example: People from the USA can appreciate an Aussie's feeling for Australia. Or a Canadian's affection for Canada. Or a German's loyalty to Germany. It's no more mysterious, some say, than love for your mother or father.

But there's a limit to that common ground.

Americans have their own culture. So do Aussies. Canadians. Germans. Other peoples of the world.

Fact: One man's home is another man's foreign turf. That makes us different. Makes us nearly—but not truly—one world.

Take USA space shuttle astronaut Franklin Chang-Diaz. Born in Costa Rica. But flying for the USA in his January 1986 mission.

"As I flew over Costa Rica, I looked down and tried to locate my country," he said. "I knew I carried into space all the dreams and aspirations of all Costa Ricans. It's a tremendous source of pride."

Costa Rican President Oscar Arias said the same thing. When he accepted his 1987 Nobel Peace Prize for his efforts in bringing about Central America peace, he did so on behalf of his citizens.

"Now I suppose most people know who we are, what are our main values, and why Costa Rica is different from many other Latin American nations," Arias told us. "[The medal] is a matter of pride for the whole Costa Rican people."

Arias: A Costa Rican first. An international peacemaker second.

Canada is another example of how much a country is like a family.

There they speak French and English. Sometimes they shout at each other. At issue: how to balance the rights of English-speakers with French-speakers—who dominate the province of Quebec but are a distinct and dwindling minority in Canada.

Sometimes it gets so bitter, French-speaking Quebec talks of seceding.

Still, the family is held together by its love for Canada. That love will never change.

That's the point Danyele Turpin, twenty-five, made when we talked with her in Montreal—the largest city in the Quebec Province. She had just returned home after traveling the world. Now she was selling glasses in a flea market in Montreal's old harbor area.

"I left home and Montreal because I wanted to follow my dream," she said. That dream took her to San Francisco, India, Nepal, and Sri Lanka.

But "I came back because I didn't want to lose contact with my roots. I just love Quebec and Canada. Now I know this is home and my country."

Just how strong is national pride and patriotism? There's a major test coming in Europe.

In December 1992, the European Community truly becomes a common market. Borders will be essentially erased. Some believe the political barriers will come down after the trade barriers. Next: nationalistic barriers.

Question being asked: Will Europe become the United States of Europe? One large Western European homeland?

Few are willing to predict. But European politicians are debating.

Like British Prime Minister Margaret Thatcher. She loudly rejects the idea of a border-free Europe. Fears Europe's independent sovereign states will lose their hard-won identity. Become one large sovereign state.

She told her European colleagues at a September 1988 meeting in Brussels that the unity should not mean that the British should give up their Britishness. Or the French, their French identity.

"Let Europe be a family of nations," she said. "We have not successfully rolled back the frontiers of the state in Britain only to see them reimposed at the European level with a European superstate exercising a new domination from Brussels"—headquarters of the European Community.

Emotions—and history—are on her side, experts say.

An example:

"After World War II there was the belief that a unified Europe could be created. That idea has long been abandoned," Hackett said. "It's clear the British will rule Britain, not France. That the French will rule France and not Germany, and so on. These countries work together on economic issues, but politically there is no indication whatsoever of a union."

And if many have it their way, that union will never happen.

But the fight for nationalism and that feeling of "I'll make it work for me" isn't only in Europe.

Listen to Bruce Mowat, twenty, of Wellington, New Zealand. An assistant cook in a restaurant:

"A lot of my friends are leaving New Zealand for Europe or Australia. They can live better there because things cost so much less," he said.

"But I've made up my mind to stick it out. After all, this is home."

*"We Are Enjoying a Rebirth"*

Spain is awakening with a renewed sense of nationhood and identity—after forty years of political paralysis under General Francisco Franco's dictatorship.

At the helm of the reawakening: proud and popular President Felipe Gonzalez.

"This is a country which is beginning to flourish," Gonzalez said. "It was traditionally considered a poor country in the European context. Now it's considered the country with the greatest potential for growth and development in Europe."

Here's why. In 1992, Spain will host:

• The five hundredth anniversary celebration of Columbus' journey to America
  • The first-ever Olympics in Spain
  • A World Trade Fair in Seville

And also that year, Madrid becomes the "Cultural Capital of Europe," when Spain becomes fully integrated into the European Community.

And along with its new international stature comes a new national spirit.

"Spain is going through a great moment in its history," said Pedro Palacios, thirty-eight, who works for the 1992 Summer Olympics Planning Committee. "We are at this moment enjoying an economic rebirth without precedent in our history."

"The place is right. The occasion is right. The year is right," said Julio Cuesta, forty, preparing for the world fair. "Spain has done great things in history, many times. We just came out of the tunnel. Why not again?"

Foremost on the agenda for some Spaniards: Letting the world know of Spain's dynamic progress.

"Many people still believe in the Spain of the tourist posters—the Spain of the gypsy music, flamenco dancer, and bullfighter," said José Luis Ortiz, twenty-eight, a Madrid barber.

"That's still here, of course, but I believe that many of us are somewhat ambiguous about all that."

Added Gonzalez: "This is a country with old roots and new branches flowering very strongly. I need to make that image known. If I can, I'll be very satisfied."

### Irish Are Fighting Back

The facts speak for themselves: Many Irish watch British television. Read British newspapers. Even work in Britain.

But the Irish have taken their knocks.

"The English blokes are always slugging the Irish," said Tom McGuire, twenty-five, a Dublin motorcycle courier. "The Brits are always looking for trouble."

But now the Irish are fighting back.

Not with guns, but with pride.

Case in point: When the Irish national soccer team beat the English team 1–0 in a June 1988 European soccer cup match, it was as if every Irish man and woman had just won the lottery.

The country celebrated from sunup to sundown.

That win, many Irish told us, was just what their country needed: a shot in the arm for nationalism.

Now, they say, let the world stand up and take notice: The Irish are a proud people and are intent on establishing themselves as such.

To their credit, a much-troubled economy shows signs of being back on track. Inflation is down, income is up. Interest rates are down, employment is up.

"Our future is bright," said Dublin Lord Mayor Ben Briscoe, fifty-four. "There's a new air of confidence."

Added Dorothy Tubridy, fifty-eight, quoting Irish patriot Robert Emmet, who was executed by the British in 1803:

" 'Let not my epitaph be written until Ireland can take her place among the nations of the world.' I feel this is the time for that."

**Despair, Yes;
Defeat, No**

While some countries bask in strong nationalistic feelings, others suffer in despair.

Take Latin America. A region with a proud—but perplexed—people. Confused and disappointed because they and their countries are faced with serious economic problems with no end in sight.

"This is a people that struggles and fights," said Argentine President Raul Alfonsin. "They sometimes feel very ill-tempered—and are always complaining."

With reason, said Ana Blanco, fifty-five, a Buenos Aires chambermaid: "Sure, we're a rich country. We have plenty of land and food. But what good does it do us? We're going backwards in this country. Money doesn't buy anything anymore."

Adding to the frustration: Many Latin Americans see their countries' promise and potential but don't know how to unlock it.

Case in point: Brazil. A country suffering hyperinflation, a huge foreign debt, and a soaring crime rate.

"There is a lot of potential," said Rio computer programmer Sergio Bondarovsky, thirty-eight. "There are a lot of things to do and if we worked a little bit harder it would be easier to get ahead. If we had less political corruption, if we had a little more planning, things would be better."

Mexico is another example. "We're a country that survives on miracles," said Jose Torres Montoya, seventy-three, a language teacher. "Even with all the difficulties and setbacks that Mexico has suffered—debt crisis, inflation, earthquakes—we're still ahead. That's a miracle, isn't it?"

Some would say the whole region is a miracle.

But one Latin American country with a different twist on its problems is Cuba.

"I will be the first to admit that Cuba does have its problems. But I also know that you can't fix our problems from

Miami or anywhere else," said Adria Santana, thirty-nine, a Havana television actress. "I'm staying here so I can help improve this country."

"Here in Cuba, you won't see any beggars on the streets," said Bienvenido Abierno, forty, a Cuban government guide. "People don't have everything they want, but they have enough."

**"Island Is One Big Happy Family"**

It's small: seventy-six square miles.

Isolated: 4,800 miles from San Francisco; 2,737 miles from Sydney; 6,262 miles from Lima, Peru.

And reminds one of TV's *Gilligan's Island,* joked Governor A. P. Lutali.

But that's the way the thirty-seven thousand residents of American Samoa like it.

"Our future is here," said student Paul Salima, seventeen. "If we go out, we shall always come back. Samoans remain close to the family."

"We are Samoan first, American second," said Faamoana Kuresa, sixty, a mother of eight children. "We teach all our children Samoan."

The U.S. territory—filled with lush vegetation and aqua-blue water—is bursting at the seams with pride. The key: Close family relationships and a close-knit island community.

"This island is one big happy family," Lutali said. "You will find no hungry Samoans here or a Samoan without a home. We help one another."

Lutali also told us how the capital and major city, Pago Pago (pronounced PAHNG oh PAHNG oh), "has more boys in the military than any other community its size in the U.S." How the island sent its first team to the Summer Olympics ever in 1988. And how plans are on the board for a stadium—if Congress okays it.

"I've never wanted to live anywhere else but here," Lutali said.

Many agree. "We don't have crime, drugs," Salima said. "All the world should be as happy as Samoans."

***"Hard Work Is
Part of Our
Culture"***

Japan, Singapore, Hong Kong, Taiwan, South Korea, and China. Titans of trade. Economic powerhouses. World leaders. Each using its own brand of Pacific pragmatism.

Take South Korea. There, a sense of "supernationalism" is developing, said Horace G. Underwood, assistant to the President of South Korea's Yonsei University.

The reasons are numerous, but two we most often heard: Hard work and anti-American feelings.

"Hard work is part of our culture," said Kang Hyung Sook, nineteen, a Seoul, Korea, fox pelt inspector.

"In Korea, we believe if we try hard enough, we can do anything," said An Een Kyong, seventeen, a Seoul gymnast. "We think 'We can.' We never think 'We cannot' in Korea."

Hard work also translates into aggressiveness, especially in Japan.

"Japanese businessmen are . . . always looking for new things," said Shinya Mizutani, thirty-four, of Tokyo, a Continental Airlines sales representative.

But many Asians also are united by their dislike of the USA's involvement in their politics and economy. Students regularly protested in Seoul in 1988 against U.S. involvement in their countries. Or against the U.S. "dictatorship," as they called it.

"There is a strong nationalist feeling in Korea now. It's reflected in some anti-American feelings," Underwood said. "But a sense of national existence, mission, is important for a country and I'm glad they're getting back this self-confidence."

Regardless, much of Asia is a world power to be contended with. And if its people are any indication, no one will be able to knock this economic power off its throne for a long time.

"I've been all over, and there's no place like Singapore—no place as good," said Singapore cab driver Ismail Yacob, thirty-seven. "Whatever a man needs in life, it's all here."

His prescription for a good life in Singapore:
"Work, raise your family, and enjoy life."

———

### Home—There's No Place Like It

———

From Cairo to Costa Rica, Zurich to Zimbabwe, people are proud of their homeland. Prepared to defend its character. Fight for its image. Carry on its culture.

"We see it all over the world," said James T. Hackett of the Heritage Foundation.

We saw it, too.

People may gripe about their country. Some may even leave. But deep down inside, there's a love for homeland in each of us that seems to grow stronger. A belief that people can work together for the betterment of their land. A feeling many don't forsake—or forget.

That's what motivates Costa Rican swimmer Marcela Cuestta, fifteen, training for a future Olympics. Like others, she could have left her country for one with a history of sports medals. Instead, she decided to stay and help make Costa Rica a country known for its strong athletes.

"For me," Cuestta told us in an impassioned voice, "Costa Rica means everything, and I would never change it for anything."

And some, like China's Ding Hongwei, thirty-two, a Beijing University English teacher, had to leave their homeland to find out how much it really meant to them.

Hongwei spent five years in the USA. Enjoyed it. But went home to China.

Why? "I just wanted to eat Chinese food, to use chopsticks, and to have my friends here," he told us.

"I just wanted to come home."

There's no place like it.

# CHAPTER 5

# Women Vie for Change

Women make up half the world's population. Some are
fighting to break out of their traditional roles and others, like
this South African woman with her young daughter, are
fighting to keep them.
Photo: Liz Dufour, *Pensacola News Journal*

WHEN Madeha Al-Ajroush of Riyadh, Saudi Arabia, wants to go shopping, she can't jump into a car and drive herself. Or even walk there. It's against the law.

And when Iman Ibrahim Abou-Boutain of Riyadh wants to board a plane by herself in Saudi Arabia, she can't do so without written permission from her husband.

It's enough to get some Saudi women talking and posing for the press—although doing so is not culturally acceptable.

"I want women to have the right to choose what they want to do," said Abou-Boutain, thirty-two, projects manager of Al-Khaligia, Saudi Arabia's first all-female company. "If she decides to work or decides to stay at home, let her do it. But let her decide."

"As a woman, I am more concerned about being allowed to do what I want:

Let me drive. Let me work," said Al-Ajroush, thirty-two, a Riyadh photographer.

Soon—they hope—it will be reality.

Their prediction: Female employment will follow the pattern of female education—start off slowly without ruffling any feathers and sooner or later it will grow.

"It'll just happen," predicted Hend Al-Kuthaila, dean of King Saud University in Riyadh. "There is a need for women to participate in the country's development. I don't think there is anything a woman cannot do because she is wearing a veil."

In the meantime, the odds are stacked against Saudi women. And for women around the world—in varying degrees.

Cultural roles, economic pressures, and the lack of available, affordable education have prevented—and are preventing—many women from growing or even aspiring to new heights.

The facts are staggering:

Women make up half of the world's population. Grow half of the world's food. Comprise one-third of the world's paid labor force.

But they receive one-tenth of the world's income. Own less than 1 percent of the world's property. And are concentrated—for the most part—in the lowest-paying jobs. That according to United Nations statistics.

There are many women who have achieved success. British Prime Minister Margaret Thatcher, Philippine President Corazon Aquino, Pakistan Prime Minister Benazir Bhutto, and Botswana Foreign Minister Gaositwe K. T. Chiepe are high-profile examples.

But there are millions who haven't.

In fact, nowhere in the world have women achieved complete equality, an international survey by the Population Crisis Committee concluded.

The five countries rated best:
• Sweden
• Finland
• The USA

- East Germany
- Norway

The five worst: Bangladesh, Mali, Afghanistan, North Yemen, Pakistan.

The ninety-nine countries surveyed—representing 92 percent (2.3 billion) of all women—were judged on health, education, employment, legal protection, and control over childbearing.

Women we interviewed confirmed the survey results:

- "What was true in ancient times between the sexes continues today," said Angeliki Kottaridou, thirty-two, an archaeologist in Thessaloniki, Greece. "There was animosity toward women, the ideal woman was childlike and if they thought me pretty, I was frivolous."

- "As a woman, I have to study harder and work harder to get the same opportunities as a man," said Naoko Tashiro, twenty-one, a Sophira University student in Tokyo who dreams of one day owning an advertising agency. "Many companies train and invest in a man but not in a woman."

- "Our marriage and family life is most backward. Divorce is still the absolute right of the man," added Nawal Saadawi, fifty-five, a feminist activist and founder of the Arab Women Solidarity Association in Giza, Egypt.

Often the battle is one of tradition vs. modernization.

Case in point: Egypt.

"The older generation of Egyptians are more traditional in their habits," said Nabila Darwish, twenty-two, a Cairo University law student. "The younger generation is more exposed to the outside world and wants to be more modern. We want to be able to live like everyone else.

"My parents want me to hold on to traditions, but I want to break with them. One of the most difficult problems is clothing. I want to dress in a certain way, like everybody else, in bright colors, in pants. But they want me veiled."

Yet while many women fight for a career outside the home, many fight for their traditional careers inside the home. They feel that change is coming too quickly—without regard for traditional values and femininity.

Three examples:

• "We're picking up the wrong side of Western society: the loose morals," said Seema Karayi, twenty-three, of Delhi, who hopes to work as a flight attendant. "When I was fourteen, I didn't know the meaning of boyfriends."

• "I think sometimes we're too equal here. Swedish boys don't open the door for girls or do romantic things. That can be boring," said Michaela Jolin, twenty-nine, a Stockholm actress.

• "My goal is to be a good wife. I want to help my husband," said Xiong Guo Ying, twenty-four, of Yanshan, China.

Fact: What works in some countries and cultures doesn't necessarily work in others.

Success to some means a job or career outside the home. To others, it's a career inside the home as a wife, mother, or homemaker. And they couldn't be happier.

Take the Soviet Union. There, a woman who gives birth to five or more children is called a Hero Mother.

She's given special benefits: She doesn't have to wait in long lines for food, is given priority for an apartment, is given longer vacations if she works outside the home, as most women do.

In China, recognition comes for just the opposite reason. Women there are given special benefits if they limit themselves to one child—to help control China's one-billion-plus population. Families with more than one child face possible fines or the withholding of government subsidies.

In other countries, like Sweden or Singapore, a woman may be encouraged to seek her career outside the home.

Here are other changes and challenges facing women around the world:

• Many—for the first time ever—are being forced to work out of economic necessity.

"The prevalent attitude is that a woman's place is in the home," said Ami Desai, twenty-one, a Bombay, India, graduate student. "But because of the high cost of living, it is becoming impossible for them to remain there. Families cannot survive without two incomes."

Said Anabel Ortega, twenty-one, a Mexico City cashier: "It used to be that women in Mexico didn't work at all. Everyone thought that working outside the home was a real bad thing. Now . . . their salaries are needed. A man's pay is not enough to live on anymore."

That need to work is bringing new, sometimes unbearable demands.

"I have to take care of my job and then after I finish I have to prepare the house for my husband," said Samya Mohamed, twenty-six, a Cairo women's clothing store manager.

"But the hardest thing is I can't be with my daughter all day. It's very difficult to connect between the work and the house and the husband," Mohamed said.

So difficult, Mohamed said, that fewer and fewer Arab women are having traditionally large families. Why? Because they "are married *and* still have to work day and night." It's too much.

Also adding to the increasing number of women in the workplace: single-parent homes—on the rise in many countries.

"I work six hours a day. I get a minimum salary that covers living expenses. I am only able to make it as a single mother because I saved money over the years for vacation," said Eva Britt Blomgrist, thirty-two, a Stockholm nurse. There are millions more like her.

• Many women are entering the work force out of choice— in increasing numbers around the world. Their goal: to climb the career ladder and better themselves.

"We want to be professionals," said Serena Ng, eighteen, a Singapore sales clerk who hopes to open a women's boutique.

She's even putting off marriage and a family life to further her career.

"I love kids but I'm not going to have any now. I work too long and can't have children. The older people are understanding this."

*NEARLY ONE WORLD*

Not all the older people. Take Singapore Prime Minister Lee Kuan Yew. He told us it's a mistake that the role of women has changed too quickly in Singapore.

One result: Men in Singapore aren't marrying the college-educated women but are "marrying down," leaving many women stranded.

"A man sees himself as 'I am the boss' in this culture," Yew said. "If a woman is of a strong personality and advises him what to do, the man—who is seen as the master—won't marry her, because she is his equal.

"This has left many highly educated women stranded. It should have been obvious to us. It was a blind spot," he said.

Another side effect of many women entering the work force: Men in some societies are playing the role of homemaker and worker.

"My father had six kids and never changed a diaper," said Peter Englen, twenty-nine, a Stockholm student. "Now fathers take a very big part in raising children in Sweden. Most men take from three to six months off from their jobs to take care of their kids."

Why the change?

Some credit the women's liberation movement for opening men's minds. Women's movements have grown in many countries and have led the fight for women's rights.

"But there is actually a men's liberation movement that urged men to share, especially in the bringing up of kids," Englen said.

• Women are often relegated to jobs for which they are overqualified.

"Girls are not so easily accepted [in business in China], so many have to become teachers," said Wang Yiqiu, fifty-five, dean of academic affairs at the twenty-seven-thousand-student Beijing University—where one third of the enrollment is women.

Same thing in Japan and dozens of other countries.

Is there hope? Yes, believes college student Naoko Tashiro of Tokyo:

"Many corporations are starting to treat women as equals to men. But they have yet to see how capable a woman is."

• Women are often put into the lowest-paying jobs.

"If I could have one thing in life, it would be a better job," said Justina Mwale, forty, a mother of eight children in Lusaka, Zambia.

She supports herself by tirelessly hammering large rocks into pebble-sized stones for use in construction. She works outside under the noonday sun alongside Lusaka's main highway—wherever she can find rocks. Her price for a half-bushel sack: $1.28.

"I'm not ashamed of what I do for a living," she said. "Even the government buys some of its crushed stone from me."

• Some women have been forced to leave their countries to pursue educational and professional interests rather than traditional ones.

Others have left because of family commitments—and don't regret it one bit.

Take Helen K. Yi, twenty-eight, of Seoul.

She was born in Korea but moved to Seattle, Washington, and became a naturalized U.S. citizen in 1980 before moving back to Korea. She works as an executive secretary.

"Moving gave me more opportunity to develop. If I hadn't gone, I'd have followed the tradition for Korean girls: Get married after college; have kids and live. Those girls are living in a society where male chauvinism is all they know. They know it's wrong, but they accept it because it's been that way for thousands of years."

"Korean husbands . . . don't want you to have a job. They want to support you . . . monopolize you," said Chong Yun-hwa, twenty-two, a Seoul, South Korea, college student. "They are generous before you marry, but afterwards they change."

• Women are demanding equal pay for equal work.

"Diligent people deserve good pay. But in [Korean] society, women don't get enough pay for their work," said Hyun Young, twenty-two, staff member of the Yonsei University Female Student Association in South Korea.

Not only in Korea. In many countries around the world.

Yet women—and some cultures—have come a long way, especially through education.

Just listen to Homi J. Irani, thirty-four, a Bombay, India, florist:

"My mother could not go to college because, in her day, women were kept at home," she said. "They were expected to marry, have children, and do little else.

"Now women are encouraged to get degrees, to become financially independent. Before, such a thing would have made parents ashamed. Now an educated daughter is a thing that makes parents proud."

However, for many women their career is in the home.

"The best part about being a woman is the happiness you get knowing you are bringing up a healthy child," said Moscow housewife Marina Malkina, forty. "I don't work outside my home. I stay at home and care for my son, Maxim . . . and do the housework."

For those aspiring to find their career outside the home, archaeologist Angeliki Kottaridou summed it up best:

"Because I am a woman, from the beginning I had to walk faster and work twice as hard to show I was able to do a job."

And she'll probably have to do more of the same in the future.

———

### *"I'm Willing to Die for My Country"*

———

It was as if we were in the center of the war.

Finally we had to call a truce—or else we would have been there all night.

Place: Ramstein Air Base, Kaiserslautern, West Germany.

Purpose: JetCapade town meeting to find out what our men and women in uniform felt about different issues.

Hottest topic: Women in combat.

"I'm as willing to die for my country as anybody else," said Air Force Captain Rebecca Meares, twenty-seven, of Reeds, Missouri.

People clapped. Cheered.

Maybe so, said Army E-4 Salvador Lopez, twenty-one, of Martinez, California, but women "would not be able to handle the stress and the pressure."

People clapped. Cheered.

The debate raged. Sides evenly divided. Women stood and said they didn't want to fight. Men stood and said they should. Different responses from the same sex.

Switch to Jerusalem. Meet Israeli Army Corporal Bat-Chen Sabbag. Her name means "charm" in Hebrew; the nineteen-year-old was carrying an automatic submachine gun when we interviewed her.

"I am a soldier, but I am a woman, too," she told us. Women don't fight in combat but "it's not a question of fear, because I would if they would let me. I can't fight, so I teach."

She added: "I can do anything any male Israeli soldier can do. We women have a mentality here that thinks that way."

Many other women feel the same. Many others don't.

It's a question that obviously will not be solved tomorrow.

———

### *Men Still Have the Last Word*

———

Old Japanese saying: "A woman is like a Christmas cake. On the twenty-fourth [birthday], she is at her peak. On the twenty-fifth, getting stale. On the twenty-sixth, no longer any good."

Some Japanese men may still believe that. Making it in the Land of the Rising Sun is difficult for women. Very difficult.

The women's role: "Stay at home, have children," said Megumi Yatabe, twenty-one, a Tokyo receptionist.

"Be soft, tender, and support the man," added Naoko Tashiro.

"It makes me mad," Yatabe said. "It's about time they turn their attention to women."

Don't expect quick results.

Findings of a September 1987 survey one year after Japan adopted its Equal Opportunity Act:

*Question:* What should be a woman's vocation?

*Answers:* Stay at home, birth of children, and return to work only after bringing up kids, 48 percent; continue working after marriage or childbirth, 14 percent.

*Question:* What kinds of work should women pursue?

*Answers:* Only kinds "suitable for women," 64 percent; everything, 22 percent; should not advance, 7 percent.

*Question:* What are the drawbacks of women who work?

*Answers:* Can't keep house properly, 63 percent; cannot bring up kids properly, 62 percent.

This survey showed more people in favor of women staying home after marriage and childbirth, compared to a similar survey in 1984.

"Women are reverting," said Teiko Kihira, sixty, chairman of the Japan chapter of the League of Women Voters. "They are letting men control their lives. The men say, 'I'll never let my wife work.' And the women are dependent on the men, mentally and materially."

Yet the number of working women in Japan has increased to 15.8 million—40 percent of the labor force, compared to 38 percent in the USA.

But most are in low-paying service or manufacturing positions. They are known as OLs—office ladies.

And women voters outnumber males by more than two million. But only twenty-nine of Japan's six hundred members of parliament are women.

Said Kihira: A woman's status in Japan is not unlike Japan's prewar "household system." The father "had the strongest power, the biggest right. He was the decision maker on management, travel, sharing the family treasure."

That system was abolished after the war, she said, but "the man remains master of the household because of his economic power. He has the last word. The husband might be the biggest enemy for the women."

But many women predicted change was coming—and promised to help lead the way in business by forging new opportunities.

"We are the pioneers," Yatabe said. "In ten years, maybe a woman could be president of a company. But now, it's too early."

---

***"I Am Not Your Average Housewife"***

She's a single parent. Mother of five. Working woman. A supermom.

Not uncommon for many women around the world. Except for one thing: This woman is president of the Philippines.

"I am not your average housewife," said Corazon Aquino, widow of slain political leader Benigno Aquino. We believed her.

One minute she's talking about her teen-age daughter's eating habits: "I constantly tell her, 'Kris, keep your mouth shut and eat it.' " The next, about foreign policy.

Yet she faces the same problem millions of other women do: balancing her work with family. Even presidents and prime ministers aren't immune.

How does Aquino do it?

She sometimes takes daughter, Kris, on some official functions, like dinners. There Aquino can perform her function as head of state and head of the house at the same time.

At a dinner at the Chinese ambassador's house where Aquino took her daughter, Kris told the ambassador that she liked Americanized Chinese food better than real Chinese food. A remark that incurred the wrath of Mom.

"I tell her, 'Kris, you can behave better than that.' And she just says, 'Oh, Mom,' " Aquino said.

Reflecting for a moment, Aquino said, "This is too much sometimes."

Aquino is not the only head of state playing the dual role. There's British Prime Minister Margaret Thatcher. She offers some words of wisdom for young working mothers.

Had Thatcher's twins, Carol and Mark, now thirty-four, been babes when she entered politics in 1959, she would have thought twice about starting a career. She wouldn't have wanted to have been away from her children while traveling throughout Britain.

"I would have felt [my children] were missing me and I was missing them. I would not have been playing perhaps as full a part [in their lives] as I should and wished to . . . being with them through their difficulties and problems and guiding them.

"And if you have a young family, it is more difficult for the woman. I'll be the first to say it."

She should know. Some motherly advice from one of the most celebrated heads of government—and heads of house— in the world.

———

**Networking in South Korea**

———

Once a month, millions of South Korean women meet to lunch. Gossip. And dole out thousands of dollars.

They belong to a *kye*—rhymes with day—a kind of Korean woman's private bank from which private dreams come true.

The women pay a specified amount of money each month—anywhere from a few hundred to several thousand dollars. Then, on a rotating schedule, each gets the month's pot to do with as she pleases.

*Kyes* don't give interest. Don't yield any more money than a savings account. But provide women with economic independence and some much-needed fellowship. This in a society where women are expected to stay at home, care for their children, and serve their husbands.

"You feel refreshed when you join a *kye*," said *kye* member Rhee Chun-og, thirty. "You meet people, socialize, boast about your jewelry and clothes, talk about your children and your husband, see your friends, and make new ones.

"We become very close. We have a saying: In a *kye*, everyone knows how many chopsticks you have in your home," Rhee added.

An estimated 80 percent of South Korean women—housewives, widows, singles, even schoolgirls—belong to at least one *kye*.

They use the money to pay for their children's weddings, education, or for anything else they desire. Some *kyes* are set up to donate to charities. Others help women start their own businesses. Sort of an underground banking system.

They're also popular in China, where they're called a *hui*. In Japan, where they're called a *tanomoshi*.

Men actually started *kyes* thousands of years ago in agricultural villages to help each other's families. But modern-day *kyes* are the domain of women.

A Korean wife is the traditional keeper of the family purse. Each week she gives her husband his allowance, pays the bills, and invests the rest in commercial savings accounts. She also probably belongs to one or more *kyes*.

"I think Korean wives enjoy saving money more than Western wives," said Chun Ae Shim, thirty. "We are always thinking about saving. And when we present our husbands with extra money, they think we are thrifty and call us lovable wives."

Kang Minjeong organized a *kye* last year. The club's thirteen members pay a total of $1,377 a month into the pot. It will run twenty months, giving some women a chance to reap the pot twice.

"Korean women believe it is easier and more safe for us to put money in a *kye* than to put it in a bank," Kang said.

Added Rhee: "If we didn't have *kyes,* banks in Korea probably would have developed a thousand years sooner."

## U.S. Women Grapple with Saudi Arabia

You can spot them blocks away. They're dressed in slacks, fashionable tops, Reeboks. Have fashionable hairdos. Wear colorful makeup. Walk without their husbands.

Others around them are dressed in long black cloaks called *abayas.* Their faces are veiled. Ankles hidden. They rarely leave their husbands' sides in public.

Quite a contrast. But a daily one between USA women living in Saudi Arabia and female Saudi citizens.

Islamic laws severely restrict the rights of Saudi women—and bring about major inconveniences for many unaccustomed USA women.

Some they comply with. Others they ignore.

Dress is the least of their problems.

"We miss the cultural life," said Nadia Naaman, thirty-three, whose husband, Sherif, forty, works for a US firm.

She's one of sixty thousand US citizens living in Saudi Arabia. Most come for high-paying jobs and a new experience. They get it.

"I can't drive or just open the door and go out for a walk. It's annoying," Nadia said. "You miss the freedom to do what you want."

She's not alone.

"Many women feel a loss of independence," said American Community Services director Catherine Jay Didion, twenty-nine. "You have to get a handle on being able to tolerate things here."

Some inconveniences for women in Saudi Arabia:

• They can't use the same recreation facilities as a man.

• They can't enter by the same door as a man in some restaurants.

• They can't be taught in person by male college professors.

Suitable dress for an expatriate woman in Saudi Arabia, according to Donna Dillard, forty, of the U.S. Embassy in Riyadh: a souk dress.

"A high neckline, long sleeves, and a hem near the ankles," Dillard said. "It's considered offensive for a woman to call attention to herself."

Not all U.S. women—and few other foreigners—comply with that recommendation.

Some practical examples: When Nadia's family visits the Riyadh zoo, husband Sherif must wait outside. Men and women aren't allowed in at the same time.

And entertaining guests even takes on new twists in Saudi Arabia. The country is dry.

Some men and women—at the risk of expulsion and arrest—make their own homemade wine, beer, and even distilled alcohol, nicknamed "hooch" and "tea."

But many women aren't so adaptable.

"We have stress talks here," Didion said. "It's the little things that bother people. A woman might need some milk for dinner but she can't drive alone to the store. Her husband is tired from the office and he doesn't want to take her. So they fight."

"One of the hardest things is finding work," she added. "Women can find work here, usually with American companies. But it's rarely in their fields, and they are overqualified. I know of a lawyer, a doctor, and a pharmacist working as secretaries."

But living in Saudi Arabia also has its advantages. Those cannot be overlooked.

"We slept one night with the front door wide open," Nadia said. Crime is scarce because of punishments which dictate a severed hand for stealing.

"And the kids can watch Saudi television from morning to night. There are no problems. No violence. No sex."

"And no *Dynasty* or *Dallas*," husband Sherif said with a laugh.

Added Didion: "There is another woman who loves it here. She has five kids, and back home she was the family motor pool. She told us she just loves not having to drive in Saudi Arabia."

### "A Lot of Brain Power Goes into This"

Feminists fight them. Fans support them. And contestants? They give their heart and soul for them.

Beauty pageants. Long a source of controversy. Long a source of entertainment.

Some see them as battles of lipstick, powder, and paint. Competitions of beauty—not brains.

Not so, argue the women involved.

Listen to the current Miss Universe, Porntip Nakhirunkanok, nineteen, of Thailand, and the woman who crowned her, Miss Universe 1988, Cecilia Bolocco, twenty-three, of Chile.

"They just don't pick the most beautiful. You have to present your best in every way: looks, personality, culture, and intelligence," said Bolocco, a civil engineer.

As a matter of fact, she said she didn't even want to enter the Miss Universe contest—or any other pageant, for that matter.

"I had never entered beauty contests because of the image they have. But when I got my civil engineering degree, people begged me to get in. I decided I had a lot to show women, with my educational field," Bolocco said.

Bolocco entered and won the Miss Universe crown in her first year of any type of beauty pageant competition. That's unusual.

And what Bolocco started, Nakhirunkanok hopes to continue.

She wants to use her popularity—and money—to help her aunt's foundation for orphaned and poor children in Thailand.

Her selection is just what Thailand needed, said government spokesman Suvit Yodmani.

"Thai women have been accused of selling themselves as sex objects. Here is an intelligent person with a nice personality who works with the poor and children—and who also is very beautiful," Yodmani told the press.

Contestants are judged on beauty, intelligence, fitness, and poise. There is no talent competition.

Miss Universe gets more than $250,000 in cash and prizes. A Maserati car. A diamond-and-sapphire necklace. Forty-year use of a Caribbean condo. A wardrobe and video system. A personal appearance contract. Even a supply of toothbrushes and dental floss.

After her selection, Porntip was featured in Pepsi-Cola poster ads as: "Porntip, the Idol of a New Generation."

Bolocco believes there's a lot to that.

"A lot of brain power goes into this," she said.

"We're great role models for girls growing up today. We are women of the eighties: We work hard seven days a week," said Bolocco—the civil engineer.

———

*"It's the Veiling of the Mind That's Dangerous"*

———

We found many women around the world to be of one of two minds: fighting to break out or fighting to keep their traditional roles.

Those fighting to break out are tired of being treated as second-class citizens. Many others reject that and say their counterparts have gone too far. It's a difference that's not likely to be resolved soon.

But as women enter the twenty-first century, they're in the midst of changes that are affecting their roles, their lives, and their destiny.

Although in some countries women may still be veiled and treated in public as if they're invisible, it's the perception of women that is changing the most.

As Nawal Saadawi, founder of the Arab Women Solidarity Association, told us: "It's the veiling of the mind that's most dangerous."

# CHAPTER 6

# The Burning
# Memories of War

War has killed some 89 million people this century. Each year, thousands of veterans and soldiers gather at Normandy in Caen, France—site of D-Day—to honor those who fought with their lives.

Photo: Callie Shell, *Nashville Tennessean*

THE Vietnam War burns inside Major Nguyen Thu like a hot bullet.

"My sweetheart died in the war from an American bomb," Thu told us. "I narrowly escaped death several times. I'm tired of fighting. But if anyone invades my country, I'm ready to fight again."

Thu, forty-two, was standing in Hanoi's Lenin Park next to the remains of a shot-down U.S. B-52 bomber.

"I was born and grew up in war," he said. "All my memories are of the war. We can never forget those sorrows and the cost to the Vietnamese. We are still suffering."

So are many of Thu's former enemies in the USA. The shooting has stopped. The pain persists.

So are millions around the world. All victims of some war. United by bloodshed.

War has killed some eighty-nine million people in this century. There have been forty major or minor wars since World War II. And countless conflicts.

At this very moment, people somewhere are living their last days—soon to be added to the body count in a bloodletting. Others are limping because of the loss of a leg on a battlefield. Grimacing from the throb that keeps an old wound alive. Tormented by the loss of a loved one. They all share the ravages of war. The dread of more fighting. The yearning for peace.

Many people forgive.

Almost no one forgets

The memories cut too deep.

I know. Rumbach, Germany, is my ancestral home. In the spring of 1945, I passed near there with the 86th Infantry Division of Patton's Third Army. Twenty-five years after World War II had ended, I returned to the area. But I simply drove around town. Visited the cemetery. Talked to no one. Memories of the war were still too painfully fresh even then.

I went back again during JetCapade in 1988. This time the war became a bridge, not a barrier. I talked with relatives about their feelings in fighting for their country. I talked of mine. We agreed that it must not happen again—that wars produce only wounded on both sides. Not winners.

Still, Rumbach's Neuharths remember the cost of war. Six died: Edith, eight, and Karola, four, killed by U.S. bombs aimed at a train. Erick, sixteen, and Rupprecht, fifteen, killed when an unexploded bomb they were playing with detonated. Richard, twenty, and Karl, thirty, killed in action.

I also accompanied French President François Mitterrand in his helicopter from Paris to Normandy on June 6, 1988—the forty-fourth Anniversary of D-Day.

More than ten thousand old soldiers were there from all over Europe and the USA. There to reflect.

Some brought pictures. Some brought medals.

Nearly all wore uniforms—replicas of what they wore in the forties.

They laughed. They cried. They remembered.

The pain. The horror. The victory. The defeat. From the distance came the sights and sounds of the U.S. Navy's Sixth Fleet Band. It was playing "Anchors Away."

One retired soldier called out commands in French. In an instant, the soldiers stood. Saluted. Looked straight ahead.

Tears streamed from the eyes of a crippled soldier who couldn't salute. He had lost an arm and both legs in the war. But he sat erect. In his wheelchair.

Officially, Mitterrand was there to dedicate the Battle of Normandy Museum. He also, no doubt, was there to remember his own war.

On June 6, 1944, he was in Paris with the French Resistance. He had been wounded and captured by the Germans in June 1940. Escaped from prison on his third try in December 1941.

He reminisced about the "immense undertaking" of the Allied Normandy invasion, which opened the door to the liberation of Europe. "It was one of the longest, harshest, fiercest battles in history."

Yes, Mitterrand, a stately, stern old soldier, remembers.

For the millions locked in the Israeli/Palestinian struggle, bloodshed is not a memory. It's a way of life. We witnessed it. Here's JetCapade photographer Callie Shell's account:

"It was Women's Day in this part of the Israeli-occupied West Bank. Several marchers clutched the red, black, green, and white Palestinian flag. Others held homemade banners accusing the Israelis of injustices against their people.

"Suddenly, I heard a whistling noise over my head. A tear gas canister clattered on the street. The protesters began running.

"Israeli soldiers appeared on top of buildings and all over the square. Gunshots rang out; soldiers appeared to be shooting in the air.

"Five women confronted half a dozen soldiers carrying rifles and sticks. The women didn't appear to be afraid. The soldiers began pushing the women. One woman, about fifty, fell to the ground, where a soldier began striking her with a stick and kicking her. But not with all his strength.

"After fifteen minutes of pushing and shooting, the confrontation eased and everyone began drifting away.

"For both protesters and soldiers, the incidents seemed routine. Today, no serious injuries on either side. No fear. Just anger and hatred."

Will it end soon? Unlikely.

Ibrahim Duaybis, forty-five, editor of the Palestinian newspaper *Al-Quds* in Jerusalem, told us young Palestinians "are not afraid. They know they may die, but still they do not fear the Israelis. I think many Israelis are now realizing it is impossible for one people to control another people."

Israeli Army Colonel Shlomo countered with a call for patience. "The one who loses patience loses the war. We have been fighting this war since independence forty years ago, for one hundred years, for two thousand years. We're not going to lose our patience."

Colonel Shlomo is the commanding officer of the "Iron Treads" armored brigade in the Gaza Strip. Shlomo is his first name. We couldn't use his last name. Israeli military censorship prohibits publication of last names of senior military officers.

Chaim Kwintnel, fifty-three, an Israeli, summed up the Israeli side for us: "Being Israeli is something mystical. If you believe [Israel] belongs to you, nothing can change that."

Safinaz El Khazendar, twenty-two, a Palestinian, summed up the other side: "There is no place called Israel. It is our land. They have no right being there. It should be called Palestine . . . [and] one day or another we will return."

That kind of determination is not unusual, according to Vamik Volkan, a political psychologist at the University of Virginia. He has studied the effects of war for more than fifteen years.

Wars claim land and lives, and "nobody gives up those things voluntarily," Volkan said. "It all remains in the collective memory, and those memories become an emotional trigger for new wars."

How do we deal with those memories?

The worst-case scenario is the Holocaust. "People never

get over it, and pass it on from generation to generation," Volkan said. "They develop the survivor syndrome, which is why Israel is a land of survivors."

But for most people, the aftermath is one of shared symbols. "We build monuments to the war. We put our grief into a certain kind of piecemeal ritualistic thing," Volkan said. That's why, he believes, the Vietnam Memorial in Washington, D.C., has taken on such an importance for people in the USA.

A war is like a death in the family, he said. "If somebody dies in the family, we mourn. Then it has to heal. It's like a wound that has to heal. But if it gets infected, you have problems."

It's a wound that's open and bleeding profusely in the Middle East. And still healing slowly in Vietnam and the USA. It is a wound that has left the entire world hemorrhaging twice in this century. It's the wound of war. The wound that, in one way or another, has scarred us all.

———

*"I Want to Tell People How Important Life Is"*

———

Hiroshima is the city of the bomb.

At 8:15 A.M. on August 6, 1945, the U.S. Army Air Force B-29 bomber *Enola Gay* dropped a nine-thousand-pound atomic bomb that exploded over the city in a fireball of light, heat, and nuclear radiation.

• 260,000 killed outright—or doomed to die from injuries

• 160,000 wounded

• 92 percent of the city destroyed

A graphic reminder: the "Peace Dome"—the charred and twisted skeleton of the city's old commerce and industry building at the heart of Hiroshima's Peace Memorial Park. Also nearby:

• Peace Memorial Hall
• Peace Memorial Museum
• Monument to the Victims of the Atomic Bomb
• Peace Foundation

- Peace Flame
- Memorial Cathedral of World Peace

Hiroshima was rebuilt. But its people haven't forgotten what happened. And they don't want the world to forget.

"I want to tell the younger generation about my experiences as a Hiroshima A-bomb victim, to let them know how important their life is, how important peace is," said Seikou Komatsu, fifty-two, A-bomb survivor and spokesman for the Hiroshima Peace Culture Foundation. "Those killed here in Hiroshima can't speak. I want to tell the younger generation that if a nuclear war takes place, there will be no winners or losers. People will just die."

Komatsu suffers from liver and lung ailments caused by the bomb.

The Hiroshima museum originally was designed as a prayer shrine. But, says Yoshitaka Kawamoto, fifty-five, museum director, "people came to bring their relics" and the museum was created.

Inside:

- Charred remains of victims' clothing
- Stark photographs of A-bomb victims immediately after the fireball
- Melted coins and glass, some mixed with human bones
- An alarm clock frozen at 8:16 A.M.
- A section of a downtown building with a human shadow burned into its stone.

Kawamoto was there when the bomb exploded:

"I was thirteen and in school. My school was eight hundred meters from the bomb's epicenter. I don't know why I'm alive. I was the only survivor among fifty students in the class.

"One reason might be because my seat was in the middle of the room. Most of the others died instantly. I fainted.

"When I noticed the circumstances, I heard some people singing songs. Some ten students were still alive. They were singing a song, a school song. In those days pupils were taught with heavy discipline, and they didn't say 'help' or anything. So they were singing. I think I joined the singing. And those singing voices disappeared. One by one.

"Many, many people were dying in the road. They wanted help. They pulled my legs. But I couldn't help them. I dreamed about this for every day afterward.

"I don't feel bitter toward the American people, but I am sad and grieving at the death of my friends. Six months after the bomb, the U.S. Army came. American GIs came to my house. They gave me chocolate and gum. They smiled. I think the smile of the GIs helped me a lot."

Kenzo Kobayashi, sixty-seven, was there, too. Kobayashi doesn't visit the memorial. Doesn't leave his one-room Hiroshima apartment. He's crippled. Shuffles on his knees from bed to television to ten-inch-high Buddhist shrine. Neighborhood women help take care of him.

Kobayashi was injured when his house collapsed on him during the blast. His wife and child died.

"I don't think the American people understand what happened here. How terrible it was. People suffering from bomb burns went to the river for relief from the fire and heat. I couldn't see the water, there were so many bodies.

"If I said I didn't have any bad feelings toward the American people, it wouldn't be true. But it's all over now."

———

**"Do Not Enter These Minefields"**

———

To Great Britain, they are the Falkland Islands. To Argentina, they are Islas Malvinas. Whatever the name, peace came to an abrupt end in the South Atlantic archipelago on April 2, 1982.

On that date, Argentina invaded the Falklands. And dared British Prime Minister Margaret Thatcher—the "Iron Lady"—to fight.

She did.

She won. Argentina lost.

Surrender was June 14, 1982.

Then the Falklands had a war to remember.

"They were so young. They looked scared and hungry. It was pathetic." That's the way Falklander Nick Hadden, fifty-five, remembers the young, green Argentine troops that invaded and occupied Stanley, the islands' capital and only major town.

Stanley, up to then garrisoned by about two dozen Royal Marines, was suddenly overrun by thousands of Argentine soldiers.

"We weren't really afraid as much as annoyed," Hadden recalled. "What bothered us the most were the guns. They were standing around everywhere pointing at us with those guns. We aren't used to that."

Kevin Kilmartin, thirty-eight, also remembers the Argentines. The Londoner-turned-sheep-farmer pointed to the rocky hills just east of his thirty-thousand-acre Bluff Cove farm.

"The Argentine soldiers were in those hills up there. They didn't snipe at us. But they ate my sheep . . . a few hundred of them."

The war was brief. But the reminders are many.

• The mountain peaks just west of Stanley became famous during the war when advancing British troops reclaimed them from the Argentines. There's Wireless Ridge, Mount London, Mount Kent, Two Sisters, Tumbledown, Mount William, and Sappers Hill.

• Falklanders have erected a seaside monument to the two-hundred-plus British soldiers who died.

• The most dramatic reminder: minefields. Argentina, in what the British say is a Geneva Conventions violation, left antitank and antipersonnel mines in fields, along roads, and on beaches near Stanley.

"Every three months, the [British] Army's bomb disposal unit comes to school to show the children what to watch out for. The minefields are becoming part of the children's artwork," said Jill Harris, an elementary school teacher in Stanley.

Most of the minefields are marked by barbed wire, red metal triangles, and oblong signs that warn: DANGER MINES.

"Do not enter these minefields," states a booklet the Falkland Islands government gives to visitors. "You may not be able to see the mines and booby traps, but you are assured that they are there. Do not touch anything which looks suspicious."

"There's really no cause here for the people to like the Argentines," said Fred Harper, fifty-five, manager in the Falklands for Fairclough-Miller, a large construction firm from Sheffield, England.

In Argentina, people are trying to forget the war. It was an embarrassing defeat for an already troubled country.

*"How Could People Do This to Other People?"*

Dachau.

Auschwitz.

Monuments to man's inhumanity to man.

Symbols of evil.

Stark reminders of the twentieth century's darkest chapter.

They both have an eerie sense of peace about them now. As if the worst has happened. And it has.

Dachau was the beginning of the road that led to Auschwitz, Treblinka, Buchenwald. Places where millions of people were exterminated by the Nazis.

At Dachau, a suburb of Munich, the memories are preserved in a museum at the Concentration Camp Memorial Site. A walk through the museum and what's left of the camp is stunning. Shocking. Sobering.

"I'm really moved and devastated by what I see here," said USA visitor Maureen Simms, forty-seven. "I look at the pictures and want to cry."

Maureen and her husband, Joseph Simms, both from Burke, Virginia, were among the hundreds of visitors—mostly foreigners, except for groups of German schoolchildren touring Dachau. In silence.

"How can people who call themselves human do this to other human beings?" asks Joseph Simms. "These people must have been sick. Hardened."

"The generation of those involved with the Nazi regime

have not shown much interest in this," said Barbara Distel, forty-five, director of the museum and memorial site. "The 1950s and the 1960s were the age of the 'great silence' in Germany about all of this, and the debate is still going on in Germany."

Dachau was the first Nazi concentration camp, set up just a few months after Adolf Hitler came to power in 1933.

"This is the camp where the road to Auschwitz began. People like Adolf Eichmann [the SS war criminal hanged by the Israelis in 1962] were trained here," Distel said.

Dachau was built to hold five thousand prisoners. When U.S. troops liberated it on April 29, 1945, the number was thirty thousand. Official records show 31,951 deaths. The real number? It's believed to have been much higher.

The figures for Auschwitz are even more grim. Between June 1940 and January 1945:

• Four million people of twenty-eight nationalities were killed. 2.6 million were Poles, including 1.2 million Polish Jews.

• Almost 90 percent were sent to the gas chamber upon arrival. As many as twenty-four thousand a day.

• The rest: shot, hanged, starved.

The effect of the death machine is still being felt today in Poland, once one of Europe's most Jewish nations. "Step by step, Judaism will die out here," said Mozes Finkelstein, seventy-seven, president of the Religious Union of the Jewish Faith in Poland.

There were 380,000 Jews in Warsaw in 1939. One third of the city's population at the time. Now about 2,000 are left. Mostly old people.

"The Jewish community [in Poland] is mostly old people now," Finkelstein told us during an interview in Warsaw. "All the young people left for Israel in 1967, when the war was declared between the Arabs and Israel. Now nobody comes back."

Auschwitz is now an empty place full of voices. There's the brick wall where the shooting took place. A simple iron beam where the hangings took place. The crematorium furnace where bodies burned on iron trolleys rolled into its fiery belly.

Candles and flowers are reminders of the nearly one million people a year who visit Auschwitz. They see a film in the visitor's center. Pass under an iron gate with its infamous motto ARBEIT MACHT FREI (Work Brings Freedom) to visit the museum housed in the two-story brick barracks.

They see Block 11. That's where political prisoners awaited execution. Or were walled up in "starvation cells." They see the gallows where Rudolf Hess, the camp commandant, was hanged after his conviction at Nuremberg. They walk through the gas chamber. And the crematorium.

They see the horrific displays in the building, labeled MATERIAL EVIDENCE OF CRIMES. A half roomful of human hair. Children's clothing. Thousands of shoes.

But what is most striking about Auschwitz is the people who are not there. Four million of them. Imagine a crowd of four million. The noise. The life. The movement. You look around. Feel the quiet. Realize that they came to this place and disappeared.

More than half the visitors to Auschwitz—65 percent—are Poles. Among them many school groups. For Poles, especially Polish Jews, Auschwitz is the symbol of attempted annihilation.

"People most often ask, 'Why? Why did the Germans do this?' " said Stanislaw Maczka, a camp survivor who now guides visitors through Auschwitz. "The answer is very simple. From the very first day of German occupation, there were independent [resistance] organizations functioning all over Poland. The Poles never accepted the occupation."

Maczka's uncle died in Block 11. His aunt, a doctor imprisoned at Ravensbrück, testified at Nuremberg. His relatives were arrested for their work in the Resistance. "Any charge would do," he said. "Simply being Polish was enough."

Why do so many people tour the horrible remains? That's what we asked Stanislawa Duda, who spent a year at the Ravensbrück camp for her work in the Polish Resistance. She had brought a group of teen-age Czech scouts to Auschwitz.

"I do it for those who died," she said. "For myself, no. I get tired. I lose the time. I do it simply because I want to convey to the young generation what I went through."

As Dachau visitors leave the museum, they pass a sign that contains a simple warning from philosopher George Santayana:

THOSE WHO CANNOT REMEMBER THE PAST ARE CONDEMNED TO REPEAT IT.

**"Bisected by Battle"**

Germany and Korea.

There are two of each on the map.

East and West.

North and South.

Germans in both Germanys speaking German.

Koreans in both Koreas speaking Korean.

Beyond that, four different countries separated by ideology, customs, physical barriers—and war.

Germany originally was bisected when Europe was carved up in 1945 at the end of World War II.

Korea was cut in two when fighting ceased in the Korean War in 1953.

In Germany's old capital of Berlin, a brick wall runs through the middle of the city. Been there since 1961. So has the electric, fortified fence that separates the rest of the two Germanys—from the Baltic Sea in the north to the border with Czechoslovakia in the south.

But it is the Wall that makes the most dramatic impact.

• Seventy-four people—more than forty the first year—have died trying to make it across the Wall from the communist East to the capitalist West.

• Five thousand have made it.

Reaction to the Wall ranges from outrage to indifference:

• "The Wall is a prison. I have a friend in East Berlin. Without the Wall, it would take ten minutes to visit. With the Wall and the checkpoints, it takes two hours. It's really silly," said Ragna Trierenberg, fourteen, a student in West Berlin.

• "The crosses along the Wall are so recent. There must still be a need and desire to get out of there [East Berlin]," said Arno Van Thull, twenty-seven, a former schoolteacher from Holland.

• "If you are a person without relatives in East Germany, the Wall doesn't really bother you that much. . . . I see it as part of Berlin," said Maria Boomgardner, twenty-six, a printer in West Berlin.

The two Koreas are on the other side of the globe. They aren't separated by a wall. They're separated by the demilitarized zone—or "Z," as the U.S. soldiers call it.

We visited the "Z." Talked to the soldiers.

• "It's scary up here," said U.S. Army Captain Don Kell, thirty-six, of Dunlap, Tennessee.

• "This is the only place in the U.S. Army where we go with live ammunition. You can't get bored. You never know when something's gonna happen," said Sergeant Richard Moberly, thirty-two, of Eaton, Ohio.

• "North Koreans are our relations. Our nations should be unified because we are the same nation," South Korean Trooper Choo Ky, twenty-four, told us at his post on the "Z."

Despite the tense calm that reigns on both sides of the DMZ, North and South Korea are technically still at war. Reason: No peace treaty has ever been signed.

And the demilitarized zone—2.5 miles wide and 151 miles long—is anything but demilitarized:

• North Korea has many of its 838,000 troops poised on its side.

• Facing them are 500,000 South Korean troops, backed up by more than 43,000 U.S. forces.

One wrong move could trigger the shooting.

*"Killing, Blood, and Grief"*

The talk today is about Afghanistan.

But there are Soviet veterans from an earlier war. The one they call the "Great Patriotic War"—World War II.

"I lost my leg as a Soviet pilot during World War II. I remember flying alongside American pilots as we fought to defeat the Nazis," Boris Kalensky, sixty-eight, a lawyer, told us in Kiev. "There was no difference between us then. And I'm glad we're returning to the spirit of friendship of that time."

Nikolai Panchenko, sixty-four, is another wounded Soviet veteran. He's a Kiev economist who lost his left hand while fighting in the infantry in World War II.

"My students want to do everything they can to prevent another war. They know we have such a great amount of armaments in the world today," Panchenko said.

"War is killing, blood, and grief," said Pyotr Zborovsky, seventy-four, a retired Kiev teacher of Russian language and literature. "It's hard to speak about it."

That's a sentiment shared by many members of the Soviet Union's "Vietnam" generation—the Afghansi. The Soviet soldiers who have fought and suffered in Afghanistan during the past nine years. Thirteen thousand killed; another thirty-five thousand wounded since December 1979. The Soviets pulled out in 1989.

Back home, many of the Afghansi have become cynical, suspicious, and disillusioned.

U.S. Vietnam veteran Shad Meshad, forty-three, met with Soviet Afghansi in the fall of 1988.

At first there were mutual suspicions.

The Afghan vets were injured and maimed by weapons supplied by the USA.

Ironically, the Vietnam vets were injured and maimed by weapons supplied by the Soviet Union.

When the meeting finally broke up, Meshad recalled, "they

all embraced me, one by one, and kissed me on each side of the face, which is their way of letting me know that I was a brother."

The commanding Soviet general in Afghanistan, asked by USA television reporters how history will judge that war, replied:

"Above all, before turning to resolve an international problem by force in the future, we'll need to think a hundred times that we better follow our old Russian proverb: 'Measure your cloth seven times because you can only cut it once.' "

———

### Island of Peace in a Sea of War

———

The Swiss have been war-free this century. A century that has torn apart its European neighbors twice.

The Swiss fought their last war a hundred fifty years ago. They have been neutral ever since. It has paid off.

"We try not to have enemies, and we can sell arms to both sides," said Langer Hermann, forty-seven, a pharmacist from Zurich.

His words echo the hard-nosed pragmatism that typifies many Swiss. "Being neutral is good for the economy of a country," he told us. "Each time a country has a war, the economy suffers. When it's over, you must begin again. When you don't participate in war, all you can do is grow."

While the Swiss didn't fight in World War II, they did have a ringside seat. Just north of Basel is the "Three-Country Corner." France, Germany, and Switzerland meet there. It's where the Wiese runs into the Rhine, Western Europe's most vital water lane.

"For me as a Swiss, this spot has a very special significance," said Gustav Trefzer, a sixty-one-year-old Basel native who comes often to look down river toward a point in the northern horizon where France and Germany meet.

"At the beginning of the war, we stood here and watched the Germans and French shoot at each other across the river," Trefzer said.

"This is the symbol of our neutrality," he said. "We Swiss believe there should be no more confrontation."

The Swiss may be neutral. But they also are armed.

In fact, Switzerland has one of the world's most elaborate civil defense systems.

"We are a very well-equipped army. We can be ready to defend our country in twenty-four hours. We keep our guns at home," said Sergeant Wirth Roland, twenty-eight, one of 640,000 Swiss who keep their arms and uniforms at home.

Just in case.

Not to make war.

But to avoid it.

———

**The Universal Experience**

———

War.

Definition: A state of usually open and declared armed hostile conflict between states or nations.

Accurate? Yes. In a technical sense.

But it omits the suffering. States and nations are made up of people. And the people do the fighting and the dying. The people are haunted by the memories.

• That's what former U.S. Army Sergeant Ted Liska, seventy, of Chicago, was talking about. He landed with D-company, 12th regiment, 44th infantry division on D-Day. "I still get tears in my eyes and a lump in my throat when I see the graves of my friends." We met him in Normandy on the forty-fourth anniversary of the invasion.

• That's what former Greek sailor Isador Vergetis, seventy-eight, was talking about. He was recalling the Nazi occupation of Greece. "All I remember of those days is the hunger." We talked to him on the island of Chios in the Aegean Sea.

• That's what Max McClain, sixty-six, of Orlando, Florida,

was talking about. After more than four months as a prisoner of the Japanese in the Philippines, McClain was sent to Manchuria. "I was a prisoner there for the rest of the war—three years, three months, two weeks, six hours, and twenty minutes. I got out in October [1945] and the World Series was on. The Cubs and the Detroit Tigers were playing. I went home to Kokomo [Indiana] and stayed drunk for six months. That's how most of us spent our back pay." We talked with him in the Philippines, where he was revisiting Corregidor and the Bataan Peninsula.

All people, of all nationalities, of all languages, have been divided and united by war. It may be the most universal of experiences.

The only other experience that may equal it is the quest for permanent peace.

# CHAPTER 7

# GIs Are Standing Guard from Germany to Japan

There are still about 575,000 U.S. troops stationed in twenty-six foreign countries. PFC Ricky Bates, nineteen, of Anderson, S.C., is stationed at the DMZ on the North-South Korea border—where hand-to-hand combat is a constant possibility.
Photo: Larry Nylund, USA TODAY

U. S. NAVY Captain John R. Condon was born in Philadelphia. But we met him on Cuban soil.

He was in charge of Guantánamo Bay Naval Base. Established in 1903. The USA's oldest military base in a foreign land. The only one in a communist-ruled country.

"This is the USA's front porch. We're seven thousand free people living on communist soil," Condon, fifty, told us. "Where else in the world do the communists have such a direct view of America? We have a potential adversary on the other side of that fence." He pointed to the seventeen-mile fenced perimeter surrounding Guantánamo Bay—"Gitmo," in Pentagonese.

Thousands of miles away in Berlin, U.S. Army Captain Scott Johnson wondered: "What would happen if we tore the Wall down?"

*NEARLY ONE WORLD*

Johnson is one of more than sixty-five hundred U.S. soldiers stationed in Berlin.

Part of their job is to man Checkpoint Charlie. That's where East and West meet. Where democracy and communism look at each other day to day, eyeball to eyeball, across a concrete wall that tears through the heart of the old German capital.

"Every East Berliner wouldn't necessarily come running over," Johnson suspects. "They have a guaranteed job, a certain security. And they could be scared of being able to cut it in a democracy."

A couple of hundred miles southwest of Berlin is the large U.S. military community in and around the West German town of Kaiserslautern.

U.S. Army doctor Patricia Zimmerman works there at the Landstuhl Military Hospital. Proud to do her bit for the USA.

"I like being in the Army, serving my country," Zimmerman said.

Condon. Johnson. Zimmerman.

Three U.S. citizens in uniform. Far away from home. Serving their country and their country's allies. Examples of the hundreds of thousands of U.S. troops patrolling the globe.

What are they doing in all those faraway places?

• Reassuring allies and reminding adversaries. And hopefully never having to "really" go to work.

• Honoring U.S. treaty commitments and defending our own interests.

"If you ever get to Berlin, you'll know why we're there," says a U.S. Army booklet on Europe.

"The Wall. The police dogs. The tangles of rusty barbed wire. The guards bristling with guns. They are a day-to-day reminder that some people in this world are not content to let others live the way they would like," the booklet says.

When World War II ended in 1945, more than sixteen million U.S. citizens were in uniform serving their country around the world.

As soldiers. Airmen. Sailors. Marines.

Most went home after victory was achieved.

Some stayed put to watch over defeated foes in Berlin, Tokyo, and Rome.

Others remained overseas to help and protect victorious friends and allies in London and Manila and Brussels and Paris.

Their sons and daughters served there twenty years later.

Their grandchildren are there today.

Indeed, more than forty years after VE Day and VJ Day, the USA keeps nearly 575,000 troops on foreign soil and sailing the oceans. And with them are hundreds of thousands of dependents.

That's more than one fourth of the USA's total military force of 2.1 million men and women. More troops than the British posted around the globe at the zenith of their empire.

• They are in Kaiserslautern and Yokota.

• In Subic Bay and Guantánamo Bay.

• In Torrejón and Crete.

• On tiny islands in the middle of the Indian Ocean.

• In secret bases in the heart of Australia.

• On aircraft carriers off Egypt, Nicaragua, Cuba, Libya, and Iran.

• In the middle of the Atlantic and all across the Pacific.

• Guarding the Sinai and protecting ships in the Persian Gulf.

• Aboard cruisers and destroyers in the Caribbean, the China Sea, near the Gulf of Sidra, and in the eastern Mediterranean.

• And they are guarding the DMZ—the demilitarized zone—between North and South Korea and the Wall between East and West Berlin.

Indeed, GIs are on guard around the world.

Take U.S. Air Force Lieutenant Colonel Tim Brady. He is the commander of an F-16 squadron at Ramstein Air Base in West Germany. "It can't get any better flying than this," he told us.

And on the other side of the world from Germany, Army Private First Class Ricky Bates has live ammunition in his M-16 rifle as he and other U.S. soldiers patrol the barren hills on the frontier between the two Koreas.

Bates and his fellow troopers keep an eye on the DMZ. "It's exciting," says Bates, nineteen, of Anderson, South Carolina.

"This is the only place in the U.S. Army where you go with live ammunition," Sergeant Moberly told us. "You get motivation. You can't get bored. You never know when something's going to happen."

"It's a maturing experience," echoed Second Lieutenant Richard Young of Tuskegee, Alabama.

Toward the east, just across the Sea of Japan, U.S. Air Force Captain Kenneth Hosterman and Staff Sergeant Stern Metheny are taking care of the USA's biggest military flying machine—the C-5 Galaxy.

Hosterman and Metheny are stationed at Japan's Yokota Air Base. Built by the Japanese Imperial Army Air Force in 1940, Yokota has been under U.S. control since 1945.

Today, most of the USA's overseas military personnel are stationed in Europe. Total: about 340,000 as of late 1988.

They and their families live, play, work and study in "Little Americas" that make the bases and their surroundings look like suburban USA.

Servicemen and women spend U.S. dollars, eat U.S.-style hamburgers, watch U.S. television and movies, play U.S. sports, and send their kids to U.S. schools staffed with teachers brought from the USA.

There are another quarter of a million U.S. servicemen and -women in Asia in a network of bases that stretches from Japan, the Philippines, and Australia to Diego Garcia in the Indian Ocean.

As World War II recedes into history, questions are beginning to be asked in the USA and abroad about our global lines of defense and commitments.

Congress frequently takes a hard look at the country's world-girdling forces. Questions asked:

• Are our forces stretched too thinly?

• Should our allies—some of them as rich as us—pick up more of the burden?

The congressional answer to the first question: Probably not. To the second question: A definite yes.

The fact is, the USA spends 6 to 7 percent of its gross national product on defense, while most—if not all—of the NATO allies spend about half that.

"We are really subsidizing their programs because they don't have to put their tax monies down to defend Western Europe," said Representative Patricia Schroeder, a Colorado Democrat, in a TV interview in 1988. "And it's our kids who are going to pay for it."

Furthermore, in many places, the welcome mat for the U.S. military is wearing thin. Take Southern Europe, for example. U.S. bases there are being held hostage to local and regional politics:

• The Turks want trade concessions and are miffed about falling U.S. aid levels. Current agreements only assure U.S. access to Turkish bases through 1990.

• The Greeks want the USA's backing for its quarrels with Turkey. Negotiations with the USA on four bases in Greece resumed in mid-December 1988 under the threat that all installations—four large bases and twenty smaller ones—will be shut down by early 1990 if no new accord is reached.

• Spain asked the USA to reduce its troops on Spanish soil and to remove a key squadron of strategic fighter-bombers from one of four U.S. bases in that country.

• Portugal, like Turkey, is unhappy over declining U.S. aid levels. It may reconsider continued U.S. access to Lajes Field in the Azores, eight hundred miles west of the Portuguese mainland and an important refueling stop for planes sent to Europe, the Middle East, and Africa.

But even outside the politically charged Mediterranean, the USA's military bases are becoming the targets of domestic political changes, growing nationalism, and even anti-Americanism among such staunch U.S. allies as West Germany, South Korea, and the Philippines.

Air accidents involving low-flying military aircraft in West Germany triggered calls for reducing or even stopping some flying exercises altogether. At least thirteen accidents involving U.S. and other NATO aircraft took place over Germany in 1988. In two of them, crashing U.S. jets killed German civilians, including four who died when a jet crashed into a residential neighborhood in the Rhineland city of Remscheid.

In the Philippines, battling local politicians have become the worst foes of U.S. bases. Nearly 17,900 U.S. troops are stationed at the Navy's Subic Bay Base and at Clark Air Base. The fate of those two U.S. installations—though just renegotiated—remains uncertain.

In South Korea, new signs of anti-American feelings, nationalism, and changing domestic politics are straining what is still a close alliance.

U.S. soldiers in Seoul and other South Korea cities have been feeling the sting of this new anti-Americanism.

"It's getting kind of scary," said Private Kevin Tisdale, twenty, of Chatsworth, California. He said he and his buddies have been called "Damn Americans" by local toughs who have also shouted "GI, go home!"

But the opposition—whether in Europe or Asia—tends to be largely sporadic. JetCapade interviews with heads of state and heads of households showed that few, if any, of the USA's allies really want the GIs to pack up and leave.

West German Chancellor Helmut Kohl told us:

"Our American friends should know that they have friends here. They should not mistake demonstrations against the U.S. for the opinion of the Germans in general. The Germans don't say: 'Americans go home.' "

***"We Have to Be Prepared"***

"It's like a small town. Even smaller than where I'm from," U.S. Navy photographer Billy Sexton, twenty-five, told us. "We have three stoplights at home."

Home for Sexton is Mandeville, Louisiana, across Lake Pontchartrain from New Orleans. But when we met him his home was Guantánamo Bay Naval Base— "Gitmo." Thirty-one square miles of Cuban soil. Occupied by the USA since 1903. One stoplight.

Since 1903, the USA has faithfully paid an annual fee of $4,085 for use of the land. Cuban President Fidel Castro, who considers the base a thorn in his side, has cashed only one of the checks.

Guantánamo is a lovely spot on Cuba's Caribbean coast. A favorite spot for sailors since Christopher Columbus landed there in 1492 in search of gold and fresh water.

Guantánamo has somehow survived thirty years of official—and often bitter—antagonism between Fidel Castro and seven U.S. presidents since 1959.

"The difference between this side and the other side boils down to freedom," Veronica Kearney told us. "Their concept of freedom is quite different from mine."

Kearney, twenty-six, was the first Cuban born on the base. Works as a counselor for Guantánamo's family services center. One of about a hundred forty Cuban exiles who live on the base and have become an integral part of its population of nearly seven thousand.

An uneasy truce exists. Minefields and a 17.4-mile fence separate the two sides. U.S. Marines and Cuban soldiers are nearly face to face.

"We have a potential adversary on the other side of that fence," base commander Captain Condon told us. "The Cubans have never, to my knowledge, seriously threatened the security of this base—but we have to be prepared."

The differences between Guantánamo and the land beyond the fence are not just ideological and philosophical. They're also physical.

Gitmo is small-town USA. There's a McDonald's and a Baskin-Robbins. Cable television and schools. Fire and police departments. A library. A mini-mart. Even a used-car lot. And the downtown area is sleepy.

But there's always a reminder—that one key reality—that makes it different.

"Guantánamo Bay is Cuban soil," Marine Lance Corporal David Whalen told us. For the nineteen-year-old from Grand Rapids, Michigan, that makes the situation very clear:

"There's freedom on this side; communism on the other. To us, the other side of the fence is like the other side of the world."

### *"I Get Us Ready for War"*

GIs in camouflage uniforms crawl on their bellies through the woods as shots ring out around them.

It's make-believe war.

It's also deadly serious.

The object: Recapture a grounded F-16, a strategic fighter-bomber.

The soldiers are from the USA. So are the F-16s roaring and soaring overhead.

But this is not the USA. This is Germany.

The U.S. military presence seems to be everywhere in Germany:

U.S. Army tanks roll down highways.

U.S. jets streak over the Rhine.

U.S. soldiers march in tiny towns built in the shadow of rotting medieval castles.

But the USA is not there just to defend Germany or Europe.

Germany is the front line of the USA's defense. And nowhere is that more apparent than in the Kaiserslautern area in the southwest corner of Germany. Fifty-six thousand U.S. military and their families live there in picture-postcard villages within a twenty-five-mile radius.

Despite the promise of Mikhail Gorbachev's glasnost and perestroika, the West remains vigilant. "In the event of war, Kaiserslautern is going to be a very, very hot target," said Chris Klepiszewski, a West German who is liaison for the U.S. Army.

Eastern Bloc troops are less than a hundred fifty miles east of "K-town," as Kaiserslautern is called.

Since the end of World War II, the USA has centered most of its European defense efforts there.

The critics back home may grumble that we're paying too much. But the tanks rumble on. And the U.S. soldiers remain alert. Young GIs feel—and know—that they are on the cutting edges.

"He and I have both been in Vietnam. We both know what it's like to look at dead people. And we never want to go through that again," said Army Lieutenant Colonel Larry Furrow of himself and his fellow officer, Major Gil Alvarado, thirty-eight, of El Paso, Texas.

"If we show those guys how strong we are, how good our equipment is, it's going to make them think twice about ever trying to take us on."

"I get us ready for war," noted another U.S. serviceman—Air Force Major Ed Whalen, thirty-six. He's the readiness chief for the 86th Tactical Fighter Wing stationed in the Kaiserslautern region.

They're all on guard. Ready for action.

***"You Can't Afford Anything Here"***

After West Germany, the largest number of U.S. military personnel abroad are in Japan. Nearly fifty thousand.

Many are stationed at Yokota Air Base northwest of Tokyo.

Their main mission: Funnel people and supplies through Asia. Fifteen thousand planes, 53,000 tons of cargo, and about 280,000 passengers a year.

On a clear day you can see Mount Fuji from the base. Yokota is in fact the "Gateway to the Pacific." The first glimpse of Asia many U.S. soldiers had when bound for combat in Korea and Vietnam.

Both conflicts are now distant memories. There are different problems now. More mundane.

During a meeting with *USA Today* reporters in May 1988, U.S. soldiers, sailors, airmen, and Marines from Yokota and other bases talked about housing, child care, finances. And just coping.

The main culprit: the plummeting dollar.

"You can't afford anything here," said Air Force Master Sergeant Clarence Robinson, thirty-nine, of Kansas City, Missouri. "Ten dollars to get to downtown Tokyo on the train. Give me a break!"

Cheri Lopez and her husband spend $1,350 a month for rent and utilities for their home off base near Yokota. "Between our rent and our bills, it takes almost one of our salaries," said the twenty-one-year-old from Rockport, Indiana.

Air Force wife Sally Spires from Terre Haute, Indiana, told us there are ways of making good money in Japan, though. Her son works for one of the advertising agencies hungry for Western models. " 'Gee whiz,' they say, 'you children are blond and blue-eyed,' and away you go."

And it's not just the youngsters. Wendell Chestnut, fifty-seven, a native of De Kalb, Illinois, is a civilian employee at

Yokota. He has been modeling for years. "They think I look British," he said.

But when Yokota residents were asked during a USA-style town meeting what they would tell folks back home if they could send just one postcard, a voice from the back of the room went straight to the bottom line:

"Send money!"

**"Get Rid of Those Jets"**

The joint U.S.-Spanish air base at Torrejón is a major irritant for Washington and Madrid.

Torrejón, just east of the Spanish capital, is one of four major U.S. military bases in Spain.

It also is home to the U.S. Air Force's 401st Tactical Wing of seventy-two nuclear-capable F-16 fighter-bombers. But they will be gone in four years. A victim of the new eight-year defense agreement Spain reached with the USA in late 1988.

The F-16s will be going to a new home in Italy. And many Spaniards—especially those living near the base—are happy.

But when we talked with them, the agreement had not been signed, and they were still angry.

"Get rid of those jets. Get rid of those nuclear weapons," retired technical consultant Enrique Mendez, fifty-five, told us. "The Americans are too pushy. They have no right to be here."

Mendez, echoing the sentiments of many of his fellow Spaniards, made it clear that while "America has been our friend, the bases are a bother to us and our family."

Housewife Aurora Jordan, fifty-four, also complained. "Our nerves are shot. The planes are driving us crazy. The Americans we like. But the bases we hate."

These statements explain why in a 1986 referendum Spanish voters chose to remain in the NATO alliance—but only on condition that the USA's military presence be substantially reduced.

It will be, under the new agreement.

U.S. servicemen stationed at Torrejón see things differently.

"It's the uninformed crowd that doesn't want us here," said Sergeant Edmund Grady, twenty-eight, from Chicago. "This base is economically advantageous. We're doing them a favor.

"The educated people know what we do for their government and their economy. They don't have any hard feelings against us. The uneducated ones are misguided."

"We're not all bad. We're here to help them," agreed Sergeant Raul Denis, twenty-four, from Newark, New Jersey.

———

***"You Get a Nervous Feeling"***

———

Guardpost Collier is inside the Korean DMZ. This three-mile-wide strip and the Berlin Wall are the most visible lines separating East and West. Capitalism and communism.

Guardpost Collier is manned by U.S. soldiers who are literally on the front line. GIs stare through binoculars strong enough to pick out the faces of North Korean soldiers staring back from guardposts a few hundred yards away.

They note every move. North and South Korea are technically still at war.

The "Z," as U.S. soldiers call it, is cordoned off with razor wire, minefields, chain-link fences, and fortified guard posts.

"You get a nervous feeling sometimes," said Staff Sergeant Keith Fowler, twenty-eight, of Muskegon, Michigan. "I know if something goes up, I'm going to be here for a while."

"You haven't got any fun time," noted Specialist 4 Mike Glessman, a sniper from Omaha, Nebraska. "We're always looking for infiltrators."

Chances of a real-life episode appear slight. But the fact that only thirty miles separates the DMZ from the teeming South Korean capital of Seoul makes the stakes high.

That's why U.S. troops roam the hundred-fifty-mile-long DMZ with rifles loaded and ready to fire.

Sergeant Hector Morin of Los Angeles put it this way:

"We don't feel like toy soldiers."

———

***"Freedom Has a Price"***

———

Forty-three years after the end of World War II, there are still almost 575,000 U.S. troops stationed around the globe.

• They serve in twenty-six foreign countries and six U.S. overseas territories.

• They live and work on 385 major and minor military bases.

• They are there to help defend the USA and its allies under the provisions of seven collective defense treaties—from NATO to ANZUS and from the Rio Treaty to SEATO.

Life is not always easy "over there." The duty can be tough.

There are strains—even hostility—in some places.

The weak dollar is a worse foe than communism is in many places.

Some countries don't want us anymore. Others think we're not doing enough.

But generally, the USA seems to be appreciated.

That appreciation was clearly reflected in full-page advertisements that appeared in leading West German newspapers in late 1988.

"Freedom has a price: Klaus has to serve for eighteen months and John is homesick for Texas," the ads said. They were paid for by the group Friendship in Freedom, a German initiative for better European-USA relations.

The ads, which included photographs of a German soldier wearing a beret and a GI in a camouflage helmet, noted:

"Both are called upon to share the burden for the sake of peace and freedom. They know why they do it."

Indeed, U.S. soldiers in Europe and Japan, in Korea and the Philippines, and other faraway places told us they want to be on the front lines.

They reminded us that they are volunteers.

And because they are volunteers, they believe in what they are doing. They are highly motivated.

Captain Dan Drejza, thirty-three, is a pilot from Utica, New York, based in West Germany. He knows he could be making more money at home flying commercially.

But there's more to it than that, he told us. "Money is not the primary reason people stay in the military. It's patriotism."

CHAPTER 8

# Communist Leaders Are Rethinking and Reforming

Glasnost and perestroika are just two of the mighty reforms
taking place around the world. At the helm of Soviet changes:
General Secretary Mikhail Gorbachev, who went out of his
way to greet Washingtonians during a historic USA-U.S.S.R.
summit in 1987.

Photo: TASS

T HE Ignatov family works hard. Has since July 1988. That's when they started their own business—a bakery.

And it's already paying off. They're taking home about $800 a month. Much more than many of the people they know.

Alexandra, forty-six, and husband, Sergei, forty-seven, run their bakery along with the help of two sons, a daughter-in-law, and five friends.

The name of the business: Bakery 612.

The place: Moscow, U.S.S.R.

The secret to their success: perestroika.

Perestroika refers to the restructuring and reform that is now sweeping the Soviet Union. Its comrade is glasnost. That has to do with how Soviet society is becoming more open. The Ignatovs and other Soviet citizens are beginning to enjoy the first fruits of this new liberalized communism.

From Hanoi to Beijing to Warsaw to Moscow—four communist capitals visited by JetCapade—a revolution is taking place. A revolution that must have Marx and Lenin—and certainly Stalin and Mao—rolling over in their graves.

Soviet President Mikhail Gorbachev is the great communicator of a new communism. His attempts in the U.S.S.R. are being emulated in many communist countries around the world. His goals:

- Streamlining a bogged-down, bureaucratic system
- Decentralizing the economy
- Introducing some Western-style prosperity

For the Ignatov's bakery, at least, it's working.

"People from all over Moscow come here to buy our fresh bread," said Sergei Ignatov, one of the Ignatovs' two sons.

"It's pretty clear to me that Mr. Gorbachev wants people to be more interested in their jobs," Alexandra said. She proudly displayed loaves of aromatny, a special black bread with a slightly sour-sweet taste that sells for thirty-two kopecs—fifty-one cents.

And then there are Mikhail Rodionov, thirty-seven, and Alexander Kolody, thirty-two. Mikhail is an agronomist. Alexander an engineer.

They now take time off from their regular jobs to sell beef at Moscow's Cheryemushkinsky Market.

"We raise two or three cows in our spare time and come here to sell the meat," Rodionov explained. They clear about five hundred rubles for each cow.

Their goal: "We're thinking about renting a farm to raise more cows," Kolody told us.

Are the Soviet Union and its communist allies becoming capitalists overnight? No. The changes and candor are not that radical.

Cooperatives that make bread and sell food are now legal and encouraged. But such things as private book publishers, beer breweries, diamond cutters, and film studios are still forbidden.

There also are other limits to the reform:

• When dissidents attempted to form an alternative political party, the Democratic Union, police arrested sixty of the leaders.

• Boris Yeltsin, Gorbachev's friend, strongest ally, and fellow reformer, was ousted as a nonvoting Politburo member in 1988 after a scathing speech in which he pushed for faster changes.

Nevertheless, the revolution of the proletariat is giving way in key ways to the revolution of rising expectations. Especially in the U.S.S.R.

More evidence:

• In the late summer of 1988, Soviet television viewers watched Michael Jackson rock 'n' roll across their screens selling Pepsi-Cola.

• Their TVs also brought them "messages" about Visa and Sony. Despite the fact that they don't carry credit cards and own few—if any—Western electronic gadgets.

• *Izvestia,* the government newspaper, now publishes ads for Western-style products. Example: Two full pages for French perfume.

• Special kiosks in large cities sell more than just *Pravda* and *Izvestia.* Since January 1, 1989, Western newspapers and magazines—from *The Times* of London to *Time* magazine from the USA—are available.

• Soviets are writing an increasing number of letters to their editors. Venting their frustration with the system. Complaining about shortages in consumer goods—from shoes to perfume and from ballpoint pens to washing powder. Expressing their views on everything from Stalin to USA politics. From the KGB to the acute housing shortage in the Soviet Union.

"We have taken everything good that capitalism has and put it into this communist society," said Generaloff Slawa, forty, deputy chairman and chief accountant of Moscow's first cooperative restaurant.

"This was started because of perestroika and glasnost," he told us. "This is only the beginning."

Slawa helps operate 36-CO-OP. It opened in March 1987. Today, it's thriving.

What do the experts say about Gorbachev and his reforms? First, no matter what their opinion, there's a historical backdrop to remember: Nikita Khrushchev was kicked out of office in 1964 because of his attempts at reform.

"But Gorbachev is much smarter than any Soviet leader we've seen in a long time," said USA Soviet affairs expert Lincoln Bloomfield of the Massachusetts Institute of Technology in Boston.

Bloomfield worked at the White House as a Soviet affairs analyst for the National Security Council during the Carter administration. He now watches the Kremlin from MIT.

Angela Stent, a Soviet affairs expert at Georgetown University of Washington, D.C., has a slightly different analysis:

"Gorbachev is probably doing much better abroad than at home. He's made fairly far-reaching proposals" in arms control and foreign policy, "but domestically there's still a lot of ferment. Growth rates, productivity, and production have all gone down," she said in an interview.

And Gorbachev faces opposition.

Not only from some of his comrades in the Kremlin, but also from some of his allies. The leaders of Bulgaria, Cuba, Czechoslovakia, East Germany, and Romania show little if any commitment to reform.

Cuba's Fidel Castro, for example, celebrated his thirty years in power in early 1989 by scorning changes and vowing to stick to his regime's hard-line Marxist-Leninist course.

"Today we say with more force than ever, 'Socialism or death, Marxist-Leninism or death,' " he told a large crowd in eastern Cuba on January 1.

"And the irony of all this," Stent told us, "is that now Gorbachev is almost a hero figure among the young people in countries like Czechoslovakia and East Germany, where the leadership is very much a part of the old thinking and the leaders are very resistant to glasnost because they fear for their own survival."

Bloomfield says that some of his colleagues are predicting that perestroika and glasnost could result in Gorbachev's political demise. But he disagrees. "I don't see that as being imminent," Bloomfield said. "He isn't going to fall off the tightrope any minute now."

Stent thinks Bloomfield is right about Gorbachev. "He's not going to be overthrown, even though there are people in second-echelon positions who don't like what he's doing."

Meanwhile, relations between the USA and the U.S.S.R. are probably the best they have been since World War II. In random interviews, JetCapade reporters found that the Soviet citizens are encouraged:

• "With our leaders meeting, chances have increased for our grandchildren to live in peace. We're very encouraged by what has happened"—Natalia Derugina, fifty-seven, walking through a park in Leningrad with her eight-month-old granddaughter, Catherine.

• The reforms "will make a difference in relations between our two countries. I think relations are good now, but they will be even better"—Alexander Makucha, forty-four, a factory mechanic in the Siberian city of Leninsk-kuznetski.

In many communist countries beyond the Soviet border, the story is much the same.

Vietnam, one of the newest, is a good example.

Vietnamese Foreign Minister Nguyen Co Thach, sixty-five, took a mini-Moscow posture during a JetCapade interview:

"Charity is not working. We are too romantic. We have taught that everything from capitalism is corrupt. This is false.

"Without capitalism there would be no socialism. Now, people who work very hard receive the same salary as the lazy ones. We are very good dreamers, but very, very bad economists."

The architect of reforms aimed at curing these ills in Vietnam is Communist Party General Secretary Nguyen Van Linh, seventy-two, an admirer of Gorbachev's perestroika.

Linh told JetCapade, "Like other socialist countries, the Soviet Union is experiencing many positive changes. Perestroika and glasnost in the Soviet Union are aimed at liberating the productive capabilities, accelerating economic, scientific, and technological development, increasing the people's living standard, and democratizing the society.

"Perestroika and glasnost are in accordance with the interest of the Soviet people—and of world socialism."

Linh's primary aims in Vietnam: more food, more consumer goods, more exports.

To help achieve these goals, Linh's government has named as its top economic adviser a Harvard Ph.D. who was a high official in the old USA-backed South Vietnam regime. He's Nguyen Xuan Oanh, "nearly seventy," who told JetCapade reporters, "Most of the reform today comes from my ideas."

His recipe: local autonomy and perhaps even profit-taking. This is especially true in what used to be South Vietnam, "where we try to encourage joint ventures and private ownership." It is in the formerly capitalistic south, in fact, where the government is concentrating its revival effort.

The People's Republic of China, tired and spent from the excesses of Mao's Cultural Revolution, hit the road to reform right after Mao's death in 1976—years before Gorbachev made glasnost and perestroika household words.

"For a long time in China we just learned Marxism. Now we want to learn Western economic theory," Wang Yiqiu, fifty-five, said. She is the dean of academic affairs at Beijing University.

And Song Baoxian, forty-five, a government analyst for the China Institute of Contemporary International Relations in Beijing, told us: "We need to keep the Open Door Policy to get correct ideas from people abroad and in China, so we can get more useful methods of reform."

Baoxian said that the Soviets like to say that without reform there is no way out. "It's the same for China. The difference is that China is going faster."

Many Chinese seem happy with what has been happening in their country. "I'm happy with the changes . . . most of the effects are financial," Hu Liang, twenty-eight, a stone carver, told us. "I have everything—a color TV, a refrigerator, video player. Growing up, I had none of these things."

Reform also is on the minds of Poles—including the leaders.

"Democratic transformations have reached very deep and they go even deeper," Polish president and Communist party leader Wojciech Jaruzelski told us in an interview in his Warsaw office.

Jaruzelski said that what is happening in the Soviet Union "is of enormous importance" to Poland. "We are doubly excited that the reforms which are currently under way [in Poland] are moving in a very similar direction as those in the Soviet Union."

But the Polish leader also advised caution and patience to his people.

"Any economic improvement is a long-term process," he said, adding that politically, "the process of democratization of public life is no short-term flash in the pan."

Leading dissident and Nobel Laureate Lech Walesa conceded in an interview with JetCapade: "There are reforms—big reforms—going on in Poland. We want to achieve these revolutionary changes in an evolutionary way—a peaceful way."

Some Poles, however, weren't so optimistic. Some were cynical. If there is reform, it's not happening fast enough for them.

"There's no spontaneity in Poland. You've got to plan ahead for everything," said Ewa Latopolska, thirty-eight, editor at a Warsaw publishing house.

And then there was Grzegorz Pawel Kostrzewski, twenty-four, a social politics student at Warsaw University. "Most of my family is on the other side of the Iron Curtain—in Canada, the USA, England," he told us. "The only thing that keeps me in here in Poland is the hope that this system will collapse."

History will issue the verdict on the reform movement. Most likely it will tell the story of how countries applied a veneer of capitalism to communism. Whatever, one thing already is clear: Change is under way. From the Soviet Union to Poland, from Vietnam to China, leaders are betting that some degree of Western-style freedom will lead to progress—not more problems.

———

***"Where's the Beef?"***

———

"Gorbachev is the right man doing the right thing—at the right time," Vladimir Pozner told us in flawless English. Make that flawless U.S. English.

Pozner's face is well-known to U.S. television viewers. He's also known at home in the U.S.S.R. There he's a commentator for the Soviet Union's state-run radio and television network.

Pozner made clear that he believes in what Gorbachev is trying to do. But he also believes that Gorbachev's reforms face an uphill fight if they are to succeed.

"There will be a struggle, but it will be won by perestroika," Pozner predicted.

"Without political reform, you can't have economic reform. The [ruling Communist] Party must cease to manage the country's economy. The Party is there to offer an ideological vision, not to run things day by day," he said.

What about glasnost? "The intellectual community is enthralled with glasnost," he told us. "It's more than most people had ever hoped."

But the average citizen, as in most countries, is often more concerned with material goods—and the Soviet Union is no exception.

"The average person's beef is 'Where's the beef?' Perestroika has to deliver in the next three to five years, specifically in the food area," Pozner told us.

"It has to. It's do or die!"

***No Tea and
You're in Big
Trouble***

Joe Steinwinder, of Gulfport, Mississippi, does business in China. Has for about eight years. Loves the country. The people.

"I was bitten in the seventh grade when I read Pearl Buck's *The Good Earth.* I've had a love affair with China ever since," he told us during an interview in Beijing.

Steinwinder and other Western businesspeople now routinely do something that was unthinkable just fifteen years ago: live and work in China—and do business on capitalist terms.

But it's still different from the West:

"There are things you learn," he told us. "For instance, if you're in an office doing business and no tea is offered, you know you're in big trouble. If tea is served but the cup is only half full, you're not doing too well."

Steinwinder, sixty, is owner and president of Steinwinder Enterprises, with offices in Hong Kong, New Orleans, and Gulfport.

He buys porcelain, wood products, and home accessories in China for resale in U.S. department stores and upper-end gift stores all across the USA.

Steinwinder says he's been in China long enough to feel the reforms.

"The changes in the last three or four years have been tremendous," he said. "I see new things every six months, and they have been more open and they're learning more of the free enterprise system.

"What you're looking at is something rare in history—a feudalistic society. It's what people saw in the Middle Ages. You're seeing a society change. It's the most exciting thing in the world."

Like business everywhere, it all comes down to the bottom line—and that's why Steinwinder stays in China:

"It's a hell of a lot of fun."

### Newspapers Are Booming

"Now people read newspapers instead of fiction."

That's what Masha Shestakova told us as she guided a tour of the Kolomenskoe Palace grounds on the outskirts of Moscow.

"Now newspapers are interesting—with all points of view," she added.

Shestakova was reflecting a fact of life in the Soviet Union in the late 1980s:

Glasnost and perestroika have not made the state-controlled press completely free, but certainly freer.

The result has been a boom in newspaper circulation and a much more unbridled press—at least by Soviet standards.

Consider the ground-breaking weekly *Moscow News,* which more than almost any other publication reflects the spirit of the new openness and candor.

"We've started to call a spade a spade," said then-Chairman Valentin Falin of Novosti Press Agency, which publishes *Moscow News.* "It is not only a result of perestroika, but a requirement of it. We had to describe the economy as it was, not as was desirable."

Falin is now an international affairs adviser to Gorbachev on the Central Committee of the ruling Communist party.

Besides the Soviet reading, listening, and viewing public, perhaps the biggest beneficiaries of glasnost have been the Soviet Union's two biggest publications: *Pravda,* the Communist party newspaper, and *Izvestia,* the daily newspaper of the Soviet government.

*Izvestia* editor-in-chief Ivan D. Laptev said circulation jumped about five hundred thousand in 1984 and that much again in 1985. It grew by another one million in 1986 and soared three million in 1987 to eleven million.

*Pravda*'s circulation also has grown, and it now, like *Izvestia,* sells about eleven million a day.

"If we could print thirteen million, there would not be a single copy left," Laptev said.

He credits diversity of news and views for the growth: "We are not censored anymore . . . I tell our news staff: Do not be afraid of anything. I will be afraid for you, but you work as your conscience says."

*Pravda*'s editor-in-chief Viktor G. Afanasyev is also frank about the changes.

Looking back, Afanasyev considers the past the bad old times. Very frustrating times.

"You couldn't criticize Moscow. We called it the city of the future and nothing bad could be written about it . . . civil aviation could not be criticized. In the U.S.S.R., there couldn't be any [airliner] accidents. Why? The minister of civil aviation was the private pilot of Mr. Brezhnev."

But can you criticize Gorbachev now?

Yes, Afanasyev said. "But we wouldn't dare yet.

"His authority is very high. The respect for him is very high. . . . We want to support this, especially in this very difficult time. . . . We try to help.

"We are the front line of perestroika."

---

**Vietnamese Businessmen Eye USA Market**

Nguyen Thanh Hung and Nguyen Van Thanh are entrepreneurs. Were before the Vietnam War. Still are—in a way.

They operate Frozen Food Export No. 1 for the government. It was once an ice-making plant. It now employs twenty-five hundred people packing fish for shipment throughout Asia.

"It has grown ten times since Liberation," managing director Hung told us. He used to own the place until the communists took power.

His partner is another old-time entrepreneur.

Their dream: shipping tons of squid, tuna, shrimp, and

other sea products to the USA—something that's officially impossible until the USA lifts its trade embargo on Vietnam.

But Thanh is convinced that unofficially people in the USA already are eating his fish.

"We ship to Hong Kong and Singapore for transshipments," he told us, smiling. "Perhaps they repack and send it to the United States."

Will the company break directly into the USA market?

"I hope someday there will be a chance."

———

**"Perestroika Is the Only Way"**

———

*Ogonyok* is a standard-bearer of glasnost.

It's a weekly magazine that has been on the cutting edge of both glasnost and perestroika.

It claims that the "Comrade Editor" letters it receives have grown tenfold to six hundred thousand letters annually since 1985.

*Ogonyok* is a combination of *Look, Life, Harper's, The Atlantic,* and *The New Republic.* Its circulation is two million, but Vladimir Nikolaev, sixty-two, the deputy editor-in-chief of the Moscow-based weekly, told us it could easily be six million to eight million if they only had enough paper to print more.

For him, perestroika and glasnost are not just something to be welcomed. These types of reforms, Nikolaev told us, are necessary to ensure the Soviet Union won't become a second-rate country.

"We simply can't live as we have lived before," he said. "Without perestroika we will be a second-rate country. We need perestroika. It's the only way.

"If perestroika wins, it will be the most significant day in my life."

What if it doesn't make it?

"I'll retire."

**Castro Still
Says No**

Time may be passing Cuban leader Fidel Castro by. There are no glasnost and perestroika in his revolution. He rejects reform.

Just four days before Gorbachev was to arrive in Cuba on December 9, 1988, Castro said: "You cannot only expect difficulties from the enemy, but also difficulties from our friends."

Susan Kaufman Purcell, vice president for Latin American affairs at the New York–based Americas Society, put it this way: "Castro hates capitalism, and while he would like Gorbachev's reforms to succeed, he opposes them ideologically because in his view they are not socialist."

And Syracuse University Latin American expert Ron McDonald told JetCapade: "Castro is frightened to death about having to do what Gorbachev is doing in the Soviet Union. I can't see Castro emulating Gorbachev very happily."

Some Cubans aren't pleased.

"If you'd stay with me for one month, you'd never want to come back. There are shortages of everything—we can't get enough meat, we can't get enough milk," said Jose Manuel Vazquez, a seventy-year-old retired agricultural engineer we met in Cuba.

Then he pulled his ration book out of his pocket and said: "See here, after thirty years they are still rationing. You can buy some things at the open market, but it's much too expensive for us. We can't afford it."

Vazquez remembered that "it used to be said about Cuban children that they were born with a loaf of bread under each arm. But now they're saying that Cuban children are born with empty shopping bags under their arms."

Vazquez and two of his friends—retired merchant seaman Bernardo Fernandez, seventy-nine, and former theater employee Enrique Ros Rodriguez, seventy-three—were quite disapppointed that the Armenia earthquake forced Gorbachev to cancel his December 1988 visit.

"We expected that the visit would help bring about changes," Vazquez said. "We've been reading a lot about what is happening in the Soviet Union in the *Moscow News* and *Sputnik* [two very popular Soviet publications whose sales the Cuban government is seeking to restrict]. We hope that some of it will rub off here.

"We have also been hearing how Gorbachev and [former U.S. President] Reagan are now good friends, while our government calls Reagan all kinds of bad names."

But many other Cubans are satisfied with things as they are. At the Che Guevara High School in Ceiba del Agua, student body president Rose Marie Ruiz, sixteen [she was elected in a democratic vote], said enthusiastically:

"The revolution has given us everything."

We also talked with many other students at the school. They spoke of being doctors, engineers, computer programmers.

"Do any of you want to be president when you grow up?"

A gasp in unison.

A chorus of "No!"

We asked, "Why not?"

"Fidel. Fidel Forever," was the chant.

———

### Reform Is Under Way

The outcome of the rethinking, reforming, and restructuring that's going on in many communist countries remains inconclusive. But it's evident that change is taking place. We saw and heard clamors for:
- Economic reform
- Political openness
- Structural changes
- More official candor

These issues dominate life in the Soviet Union, China, Poland, Vietnam, and to one degree or another, most other communist countries.

We found a variety of voices regarding the reforms:

• A. A. Fyodorov, forty-five, is the chairman of a cooperative restaurant in the Soviet capital. "Gorbachev is giving us the opportunity to breathe free. . . . We're ready to go to the barricades for him," he told us. "But we've only inhaled once and the main point is that the pipeline with the oxygen is not interrupted."

• Bette Bao Lord, forty-nine, was born in Shanghai and raised in Brooklyn, New York. The Chinese, she told us in Beijing, "have found a new sense of expression. People are able to be family again, able to be friends again. Now people are analyzing for themselves. If China is to succeed with the reforms, they have to analyze for themselves.

"When you have a country with one billion people speaking with the same voice, it's dangerous." She is author of the best-seller *Spring Moon* and wife of the former U.S. ambassador to China, Winston Lord.

• "There's more optimism now," said Vladimir Vinogradov, thirty-one, a heavy equipment operator in the Russian city of Lipetsk.

• Not so, countered Vera Gorayachev, twenty-six: "We don't feel any improvements yet as a result of perestroika." She and her new husband, Yevgeny, told us that as of yet "we can only dream of a flat of our own."

• Chen Gen Bao, thirty, is a factory supervisor in Shanghai. "How much better off am I in today's China? When my parents were young, they lived in the dark ages. We own a color television set, a refrigerator, a washing machine, and three bicycles."

• Nicolaj Ivanyutenko, fifty-one, is chief engineer at a heavy industry plant in Novosibirsk in Siberia. "We hope perestroika will work," he told us. If it does, he said, "our life is going to be much more interesting than it was."

• Mirek Oszczygiel, thirty-six, is a Ford representative in Warsaw. "The economic situation isn't very good in Poland," he told us. "Something has to be done . . . but I'm not sure how successful the government's economic reforms will be."

• But in the Soviet Union, factory worker Alexander Makucha told us in the Siberian city of Leninsk-kuznetski: "Gorbachev's reforms will make life better for us."

• "I wrote a poem about perestroika. I'm for it with all my heart," Maria Kondrachina, fifty-seven, told us in Novosibirsk. She's a "floor lady"—a floor attendant—at one of the local hotels there.

But all of this is tempered by caution, skepticism, frustration. And impatience.

Polish leader Jaruzelski reminded us that reform takes time. "If we are to have a better tomorrow," he said, "today must be perhaps more difficult."

But Barbara Surmacz and other Poles are skeptical. They have all heard that before. Asked Surmacz, twenty-seven, a Warsaw dressmaker and model:

"When is tomorrow?"

# CHAPTER 9

# Making Time to See
# the Sights

People around the world love to play. To relax and recharge.
Forget and have fun. One of the most exciting and romantic
places to do that: Rio's famed Copacabana Beach.
Photo: Joel Salcido, *El Paso Times*

TOURIST Craig Quenstedt of Houston, Texas, has wanted to shoot wild game for a long time. He finally got his chance on the northern edge of Kenya's Serengeti Plain.

In the distance, he spotted his prey: A baby Thompson gazelle peacefully stretching its small back legs. Pointing its nose to the sky.

Quenstedt's driver quietly inched his minibus—full of equipment—toward the unsuspecting animal.

Quenstedt stuck his head out of the bus. Loaded. Aimed. Waited. Quietly. Without even blinking an eye. Then, in a burst of excitement . . .

Click. Click.

"I got him!" screamed the oil drilling company executive. "I got him right in the middle of a stretch."

The animal—seemingly unscathed—dashed away for its life.

Quenstedt—the proud hunter—watched and rejoiced in his shoot. It was clean. Quick. On target.

He lowered his 35-millimeter camera with telephoto zoom lens and pulled back into the bus.

"What now?" asked the guide behind the wheel.

"Cheetah!" said Craig's friend Normand Grenier of Houston, Texas. On they drove.

Quenstedt and Grenier are two of the more than one thousand tourists swelling the 653-acre Maasai Mara Game Reserve in Kenya each day. For a peek—or picture—of elephants, lion, gazelles, and dozens of other animals.

They're also two of millions vacationing each year. In Rio and Rome. In Barcelona and Bora-Bora. And thousands of other destinations around the world. They go:
- To sun and soak. Shop and sail.
- To hike and bike. Dance and dine.
- To relax and refresh. Frolic and forget.

We are a world that loves to play—and more and more of us seem to have an opportunity to do so.

We save all year to shop from sunup to sundown in sale-saturated Singapore.

Exercise and watch our weight—to don dental floss bikinis on Rio's trendy Copacabana Beach.

And sweat in mud-filled fields to work on a vacation sheep farm in rainy New Zealand.

"We really need a holiday where we can slow down," said Roy Hunt, an engineer from England vacationing with his wife, Pat, a marriage counselor, in Tralee, Ireland. "We both have jobs where we are racing all day long."

So the Hunts rented an Irish draft horse and a gypsy caravan and are slowly traveling, like gypsies, around Ireland. "You can really relax," Hunt said.

That's exactly what Leslie Johnson, thirty-four, of Pascagoula, Mississippi, was after.

"I've got three little ones, so I'm constantly on the run," Johnson said, tanning on crystal-white sand in the South Pacific. "I'm here to get away. This is my time."

Get away she did. To Bora-Bora in the South Pacific.

Expensive? Yes. Suntan lotion is $18 for small bottle, accommodations over $300 a night. But what an exquisite getaway.

For Johnson and other vacationers, tourism means relaxation and fun. But it also means big business—with a capital *B*—for countries around the world.

Countries count on it. Businesses bank on it:

• In Acapulco alone, five million tourists pumped an estimated $2.5 billion into the Mexican economy in 1988.

• In Italy, fifty million tourists visit annually from around the world, 1.8 million in 1987 from the USA.

Italy is the USA's second most popular European destination—just behind the United Kingdom and ahead of France and Germany. Europe is the top choice for the world's vacationers.

We are also traveling more. International airlines carried eighty-eight million passengers the first half of 1988—6 percent more than the same period in 1987.

Reason: Increased air traffic to and from the Far East, according to the International Air Transport Association.

Although U.S. residents are the world's leading tourists, that will change by the year 2000, says the London-based Economist Intelligence Unit.

Germans and Brits will surpass U.S. tourists in the number of overseas trips taken, the total number of tourists going abroad, how long they stay, and how much they spend.

The report says U.S. citizens will not travel less—but people from other countries will travel more.

It's no wonder many heads of state touted their country's sites and spectacles in JetCapade interviews. Two examples:

• Italian Prime Minister Ciriaco De Mita: "If you really want to see how the world developed through time, you have to come here. We have something extra."

• Australian Prime Minister Robert Hawke: "The concept of joining us and throwing a shrimp on the barbie is not just advertising talk, it does reflect a sort of openness of character. It is real."

Governments worldwide in countries large and small are pumping millions into tourist accommodations and attractions to bring in big bucks.

And tourism is not just for the rich anymore—thanks to more economical jet travel and strengthening economies.

"More and more big hotels are full of working class people," said Roger Michetti, fifty-three, of St. Laurent du Val, France.

But tourism—like most businesses—has its ups and downs. The reasons:

• Terrorism: Greece and Israel have suffered setbacks from news reports of terrorism.

Greek tourism from the USA dropped to 200,000 people after 1985 and 1986 terrorist attacks. But officials hope for 370,000 USA tourists in 1989.

"Americans started thinking of Greece as being in the Middle East," said Nicholas Skoulas, Greece's deputy minister of tourism.

Greece has launched a $3 billion–plus renovation and a $3 million public relations campaign to get tourists back.

Israeli officials hoped for 1.7 million tourists in 1988. But, in part because of the uprisings in the occupied West Bank, they had to settle for under 1.5 million. Hotels—which usually run at 65 to 75 percent occupancy—were down to 50 percent.

"Are we losing money? You bet," said the Reverend Dave Kelley, a Baptist pastor from Morris, Oklahoma, who had expected a group of thirty-five tourists to the Holy Land. He got fourteen.

"Let's put it this way: The phones are not ringing like they used to," said David Shoham, sales and marketing manager for Jerusalem's Hyatt Regency. "This year should have been the biggest ever and it's not going to happen."

• Thrifty tourists: The fallen U.S. dollar and foreign currencies has stifled tourism to Europe and other popular destination points.

"Tourist income has been going down for the past two years. More people are coming, but they are spending less," said Marcelo Pasetti, twenty-four, feature writer for *La Capital,* an Argentine newspaper in Mar del Plata, the country's most popular beach resort.

"Many just come for a weekend, bring their own food, and are on a tight budget, spending about $14 a day," Pasetti said.

Added Adriano Manopulo, fifty-six, a Bank of Rome executive: "The weaker dollar certainly has benefited the Italian economy, but it hasn't been good for tourism—especially from America."

One country that has benefited from weaker foreign currencies: Japan.

We found Japanese tourists in nearly every country and corner we were in—even thirty feet underground in a Zurich, Switzerland, bomb shelter.

For many Japanese, it's cheaper to travel abroad than to stay home.

But many tourists visiting Japan—the land of rising costs—wish they had stayed at home.

Dinner for two is about $450 at a fashionable Tokyo restaurant; cab ride from airport, $154; nail polish, $30.

The prices have caught many tourists by surprise.

"Cup O' Noodles is what I live on," said tourist Dwayne Mackie, eighteen, of British Columbia.

• Overuse: Overzealous tourists and increasing numbers of tourists' vehicles—even hot-air balloons—are scaring wildlife and damaging the environment in many parts of the world.

"Sometimes I see twenty drivers around one animal," said Simon S. B. Makallah, senior game warden at Kenya's Maasai Mara Game Reserve.

Added Perez Olindo, Kenya's director of wildlife conservation and management: "I don't think anybody can deny that where you have human beings, you must have a problem."

But tight budgets, crowds, and fear of terrorism are not stopping everyone. In interview after interview, people told us that, more than ever, they need—and are making time for—their vacations.

"If you have a busy job, you need to wash out your brain," said Marie-Louise Grettve, a Stockholm doctor vacationing in Ireland.

Added Audrey Rouse, sixty-four, from Walton-on-Thames,

England, visiting the Falkland Islands: "It's now or never, before it's too late."

———

***"The Waves Knock It Right Off"***

———

The work begins months before they ever begin their vacation. They run. Diet. Do aerobics. Visit tanning salons. Anything for the perfect body.

Finally, they arrive. And they still stick out.

"I looked like a piece of cheese compared to them," said Swiss tourist Noel Zehler, thirty-two. "I was so white and my bathing suit was so big. I was hiding myself behind rocks to get some sun."

He's not alone.

These are Rio's Copacabana, Ipanema, and Leblon beaches. World-renowned for their bronzed Brazilian bodies—men and women. And for the song, "The Girl From Ipanema."

Here, "dental floss" bikinis are "in." They're the first cousin to the G-string. Revealing more flesh than they cover. Leaving little to the imagination.

Men, too, have their own version. Or they wear fashionable surfing suits.

"I expected a bikini but not this. . . ." Zehler said.

"It's shocking—but in a nice way," added Costa Rican Roxana Teran-Victory, twenty-eight. But she refused to put on the dental floss. "I would feel overexposed!" she said.

Other beach criteria: the perfect tan and body.

"What's in style for men is an athletic body," said Rio college student Marcia Leal, twenty-seven, in her dental floss. She was surrounded by athletic bodies.

Simply put, "The beach is a fashion show," Zehler said. "Everyone walks around to see, be seen, and flirt. There's a special mentality here found nowhere else."

Natives agree.

"The sensation of the beach is looking at a girl in a bathing suit like that," said Wilson de Mesquita, twenty, a Rio computer programmer, pointing to a curvaceous young woman. "I think men in general like girls in bathing suits like that."

More than a few sets of eyes were going to be on Hampshire, England, tourist Wendy Beacher, forty, when she hit Copacabana in her red dental floss.

"I'm not adverse to trying it," she said before putting on her suit. "You got to do what the natives do. Besides, Europeans are used to topless beaches."

"I'm doing this for me," Beacher told us. "There are too many stunning beauties to show off. If you're over thirty, you're not as voluptuous as the seventeen-year-olds."

Typical routine for tourists: "They buy the dental floss and use it every day. But once they go back home, they never wear it again," said Elaine Paes Barreto, forty, co-owner of Germany's, a bikini manufacturer and store in Rio.

More typical tourist routines: Constantly taking pictures of beachgoers and running from beach blanket to ocean in their dental floss—hoping no one will notice.

"Never run into the water with this on," said Michele Liberti, sixteen, pointing to her green-and-blue dental floss and shaking her head at a tourist running toward the water. "The waves knock it right off."

But tourists aren't the only ones a little embarrassed by the dental floss.

Said Eugenia Cukier, seventy-three, a retired Rio housewife: "These new swimsuits that show everything are nice but there's no charm to them. Fifty-three years ago, we would ride the bus and men would go wild trying to get a glimpse of our ankles. Now you see everything without even looking."

**"The Prices Knock You Silly"**

The Japanese call it *endaka:* the almighty yen. Tourist's translation: Highway robbery.

Just ask Charles Anderson of San Francisco. He spent $450 for dinner for two at a French restaurant in the resort town of Hakone.

Or Keith Sanders of Honolulu, who shelled out $15 in Tokyo for one shot of cognac. "Damn," said Sanders, twenty-five. "It almost makes you want to quit."

Japan's strong yen has nearly crippled the USA dollar. Badly curtailed the buying power of other major currencies.

No wonder. Tokyo is the most expensive city in the world to visit, according to the *Consumer Reports Travel Letter.* One day in Tokyo for two people—in a moderately priced double hotel room, three meals, transportation, and incidentals—costs $460. That's $91 more than runner-up's Paris and $202 more than New York.

Finding a USA tourist not on an expense account is as rare as snagging a bargain at a Ginza Department Store. The dollar gets about 125 yen. Business travel remains strong, but tourism is suffering.

"We see businessmen, not tourists," said Dorothy Guzzwell, forty-five, a United Airlines flight attendant on the Seattle-Tokyo route. "There aren't the little old ladies coming over on shopping sprees. There are no bargains here."

That first brush with Japanese prices can be a shocker: $154 for a one-hour cab ride from Tokyo's Narita Airport to downtown Tokyo; $80-a-person dinner in a traditional Japanese restaurant; $4 for a cup of coffee in the deluxe Okura Hotel.

Gut reaction from most tourists: "Ouch," said Linda Babcock, thirty, from Tallahassee, Florida.

Maxine Moore, seventy, of Danbury, Connecticut, also has felt the pinch.

She stayed with a friend for a month in Tokyo. Spent more than $1,000 on gifts and had only trinkets to show for it: key chains, sake sets, and trays.

Shops catering to foreigners also are feeling the effects.

At Hiyashi Kimono in Tokyo, business was down 10 percent in 1988 from the previous year, even though kimono prices have been kept deliberately low to attract tourist business.

But when you look at anything other than kimonos, "the prices knock you silly," said Margaret Egan, eighty-two, from New York.

A sampling:

• Cover charge for a Tokyo nightclub in trendy Roppongi district: $156

• One beer at Hard Rock Cafe: $8

• One kilogram of beef (2.2 pounds): $243.90

• Two muskmelons: $165.85

• One pound of cherries: $120.95

• Five peaches: $40.65

• One two-pound box of Velveeta cheese: $10.81

No wonder some enterprising tourists have been known to buy a pack of toothpicks (81 cents) and make a lunch out of the free samples of food at the Ginza Department Stores.

Rachel Baer, twenty-one, working at the Tokyo Disneyland, has also found a way around the high costs: She lives on corn and tuna.

A bit of advice from David Scott, twenty-seven, working in Tokyo: "I stopped thinking in dollars a long time ago. If you do, it makes your head hurt."

### *"This Is Paradise"*

It's a tourists' dream come true.

Just ask Jean Moore, fifty-seven, of Rancho Palos Verdes, California: "I've waited thirty-three years to come here. This is just like a Hollywood movie—only prettier."

This is Bora-Bora. One of 130 Tahitian islands. Formed from a volcano. Named after a drumbeat. Made famous by French painter Paul Gauguin.

Called the most beautiful, most secluded, most exotic of the French Polynesian islands in the South Pacific.

"The coconuts really fall off the palm trees and the women are beautiful," said British tourist James McLeod, forty-two, a management consultant. "Your first impression: This is paradise—especially if you're from a cold climate."

No one leaves the island disappointed. Even the natives from Tahiti come here to unwind.

"The tourists call my home paradise," said Tahitian resident Olga Perillaud, forty. "But we come to Bora-Bora when we need to get away."

This exotic island sanctuary (population 3,700) is the playground for the rich and famous, like Charlton Heston, Diana Ross, and Ringo Starr. It was even featured on the USA TV show called *Lifestyles of the Rich and Famous.*

Leslie Johnson, of Pascagoula, Mississippi, watched the show. Weeks later, she was in Bora-Bora, covered in suntan lotion No. 29.

"Have you ever seen a place more gorgeous?" she asked, sunbathing on the sand.

Tourists come here to swim in the crystal-clear blue water—clothes optional. Snorkel among the rainbow-colored fish playing hide and seek in the emerald-green reefs.

Lie peacefully on the snow-white sand under the noonday sun. Sail into orange sunsets that light up many an artist's canvas.

Or simply fall fast asleep in the shade of a dark green palm tree—secluded from the rest of the world.

The attitude in Bora-Bora, according to McLeod: "Take your shoes off. Walk barefoot in the sand. Take it easy."

And Tahitian officials want to keep it that way. They're reluctant to sell land titles, so development on the island is kept at a minimum.

"This is not the place to go for dinner and dancing," said Amy Heller, twenty-four, honeymooning with her husband, Warren, twenty-seven. Both are from New York.

"You're at the end of the earth. But the beauty of this place surpasses anything we've ever seen—including the Caribbean," she said.

But paradise can cost a pretty penny.
- Suntan lotion: $18
- Hotel bungalows: up to $400 a night

That doesn't seem to deter lots of folk.

"Everybody who has ever been there wants to go back," said author James Michener. Bora-Bora is "the most beautiful island in the world."

**Liechtenstein Couldn't Be Happier**

It's an enchanting little fairy tale kingdom.

With a Prince Charming. Camelotlike castle. Picturesque countryside. And 27,400 faithful subjects. All of whom live peacefully on 61.8 square miles.

But one day this fairy tale kingdom was invaded by thousands of tourists—and little Liechtenstein hasn't been the same since.

Tour buses and rental cars jam the one-lane road through downtown Vaduz, the capital. People pack the post office. Crowd the card counters. Replete the restaurants. Savor the souvenir shops.

Over seventy-five thousand of them a year. Most from Germany, Switzerland, the USA, the United Kingdom, Ireland, and France.

And Liechtenstein's government couldn't be happier.

The tourists come to see—and photograph—one of the world's smallest countries. Main subjects: castle and mountains.

Get their passport stamped—with real postage stamps. Price: One franc ($1.50).

"It's a sentimental thing," said Venezuelan tourist Carmen Gomez, thirty-six. "A typical tourist remembrance that your friends can look at."

Buy some of Liechtenstein's world-renowned postage stamps. And send those postcards. Tourists can be seen busily writing all over the country. It's not everyone who writes—or receives—a postcard from Liechtenstein, tourists told us repeatedly.

"Prince Hans Adam runs his princedom as a business, and it works," Gomez said. "It's clean, orderly, and well run."

Stamp sales alone bring in $18 million a year, said Hugo Meier, sixty, director of the state Philatelic Service.

"We don't have any embassies," Meier said. "Our ambassadors of the country have been the stamps."

Up to twenty-five new stamps are issued a year with colorful, elaborate designs. Besides sales to tourists, Liechtenstein also has over a hundred thousand regular stamp subscribers, most of whom are foreign.

But, said Berthold Konrad, forty-nine, national tourist office director, there is much more to this fairy tale kingdom.

Liechtenstein also is known for its manufacture of false teeth and its banks full of foreign accounts. Unofficial estimates: Over forty thousand companies are registered in Liechtenstein.

It lies on the east bank of the Rhine River. Tucked in a mountain valley between Switzerland and Austria. Surrounded by breathtaking views of the snow-capped Alps.

It's "a Switzerland and Austria in miniature," said Konrad.

"If in Switzerland, you have to go all over three hundred kilometers; here you can do it all in a quarter of an hour."

But he wants you to stay longer.

"In Germany and Switzerland, they say you can go through Liechtenstein and in twenty minutes you've seen it," Konrad said.

"We feel sorry about that. Liechtenstein could offer much more than a stop at Vaduz and a meal. If I have to show Liechtenstein to someone from the outside, it takes me three weeks."

Most people stay for three hours. And—except for the castle—have a hard time distinguishing Liechtenstein from its neighboring countries.

But officials don't seem to mind too much.

Tour groups promote this pint-sized principality as a stop between Lucerne, Switzerland, and Innsbruck, Austria.

"From the way of life, we are more Austrian. In the way of business, we're more Swiss," Meier said. "But the best of the sandwich is in the middle."

"There's a difference," said Australian tourist Toby Hartley, twenty-three, after getting his passport stamped. "But it's hard to define."

---

### *"Looking for Those Who Can Spend Money"*

Austria to Australia, Singapore to Saudi Arabia. When it comes to tourism, these countries—and most of the others around the globe—see green, silver, or gold.

They all want your money—and will do about anything to get it.

They use multimillion-dollar ad campaigns. Offer lucrative travel packages. Escort you to tax-free tourist shopping. And build theme parks and attractions for every imaginable taste.

Said Greece's Deputy Minister of Tourism Nicholas Skoulas: "We're looking for those who can spend money."

Even Saudi Arabia, Cuba, Vietnam, and the Falkland Islands—not normally known as tourist attractions—are trying to enter the market.

After years of isolation, Vietnam started promoting itself in 1987. It's first tourist brochure was glossy, but somewhat tentative: "We don't promise you wonders. We simply propose to show you a country in all its human and geographic diversities."

By the end of 1988, hundreds of USA tourists had taken Vietnam up on the offer—to see the "diversities" and, no doubt, to reflect on a painful chapter in U.S. history.

Falklanders are trying to rescue a tourism industry that was devastated by the 1982 war between Great Britain and Argentina.

"We're looking for people who are primarily interested in a pretty much untouched wildlife environment," said Graham Bound, thirty-one, managing director of Falkland Islands Tourism.

Before the war, business was steady, with tourists coming over from Argentina, Brazil, and other South American countries.

Bound wants the South Americans to return. He also wants tourists from the USA. "We're getting a lot of interest and even some American clients," Bound said.

"It's a completely unspoiled environment," Bound said, touting his homeland's attractions. These islands "have a completely different type of geography. It's one of the few sub-Antarctic islands people can actually get to."

Many countries that already have a healthy tourism industry are trying to do even more.

Take Singapore. It's safe. Clean. Beautifully landscaped. The phones work. The water is drinkable. The hotels, luxurious.

Twenty years of modernization has brought Singapore new housing, new industry, and a new subway. But along the way, local color got accidentally erased.

"Shopping is not enough," said Pamelia Lee of the Singapore Tourist Promotion Board.

So the government plans to rebuild the very districts it cleared just a few years ago.

Planned: preservation of Little India and Arab Street, two ethnic areas; restoration of Bugis Street for food vendors (but minus the transvestite prostitutes who once called the street home); construction of a maritime museum; and expansion and development of a theme park based on Chinese mythology.

Said Lee: "To bring back life is not easy." But for the sake of culture and dollars, Singapore is giving it a try.

Here are what some other countries are doing:

• China: For those on the rush through the Far East, there will be Shenzhen's Beautiful China Project. It will recreate China's most famous sites on a small scale—a very small scale.

The 3,750-mile Great Wall will be reduced to 3,900 feet.

The giant Loshen Buddha will be shrunk to a twenty-seven-foot-tall replica.

Officials hope to lure some of Hong Kong's 4.5 million visitors and China's 870,000-plus tourists.

After you've been to Shenzhen, officials say, there's no real need to visit the real-life monuments and attractions these replicas are based on.

• U.S.S.R.: The Kremlin, Red Square, and Soviet Georgia must be too good to pass up.

At least, that's what the Soviets have concluded by their overwhelming number of visitors.

They've had to turn away thousands of tourists for lack of sleeping space. Those who are lucky to find room at the inns complain of poor service and outdated facilities.

"All the perestroika tendencies are very interesting to people abroad," said Victor Makagonov of Intourist, the state tourism agency. "We would like to receive all the tourists who would like to come, but there is a big 'but.' "

Intourist is now building thirty new hotels and renovating thirteen more. That means twenty-two thousand to twenty-three thousand new beds by 1990 and lots more rubles for the Russians.

• Greece: This country is the "European's European Vacation" choice, Greek ads say.

But the Greeks want more people from the USA to visit their islands.

Americans spend an average of $1,250 per person. That's two and a half times more money than those from other countries.

To capitalize on the U.S. tourists—and to continue to attract the Europeans—Greece is constructing higher-class hotels with golf courses, spas, casinos, ski resorts, marinas, and additional airports.

They hope it works.

"Americans love to emulate the Europeans. They consider Europeans more knowledgeable about living," Skoulas said.

He hopes to soon find out if his theory is true.

———

**Tourism
Around the
World**

———

Whether it's a romantic weekend away from home or an exotic safari through the wilds of Africa, we are a world that loves to play.

Work hard. Play hard. That's a theme we often heard.

Here are some memorable JetCapade impressions of playgrounds around the world:

• Fiji: Tourism is on the rise again following two 1987 coup attempts. Occupancy rates, which had slipped to 35 percent, are back up to 50 percent.

• Tahiti: Natives leave the island on weekends to escape tourists. The island attracts a hundred fifty thousand tourists a year.

• Saudi Arabia: The country wants to lure a million tourists a year with its new public relations campaign. Will stress its beauty, folklore, and one national park.

• Vietnam: USA tourists crawl through old Viet Cong hiding tunnels. The country wants more tourists but can't house them comfortably.

• Cuba: Foreigners flock to the Tropicana Nightclub—Havana's biggest attraction. The country is preparing for the 1991 Pan American sports games. Hopes to convince the world that communism has produced a prosperous country—contrary to news reports.

• Singapore: Over two thousand Singapore slings are served daily at the Raffles Hotel—once home to famed writers and now to busloads of Japanese tourists.

• Israeli occupied West Bank: Tourists jam Old Jerusalem and Bethlehem to visit Biblical sites—despite threat of Palestinian-Israeli bloodshed.

• Japan: Tourists and businesspeople dine with real Japanese families for a taste of home-style sushi—compliments of the tourist board. No charge. Available to all visitors.

• England: Foreigners flock to Abbey Road and Liverpool to walk the steps of the Beatles. Stand outside Buckingham Palace for a view of the Queen, Prince Charles, or Lady Diana.

• Ireland: Two hundred fifty thousand tourists a year hang nearly upside down to kiss the legendary Blarney Stone for good luck.

• Philippines: Thirteen thousand tourists—many Filipino—tour the former home of Imelda and Ferdinand Marcos for a glimpse of the excess and eccentricity that made the former leaders infamous.

• Egypt: Magical, mystical pyramids and the Sphinx lure millions despite the monuments' ailing structures.

• France: The Eiffel Tower, the Arc de Triomphe, and the Louvre Museum—only three of limitless possibilities for honeymooning tourists.

All places to relax and recharge. Forget and, in the words of Costa Rican tourist Roxana Teran-Victory, found sunning herself on a Rio beach, "have fun. Everyone needs some time to cut everything out."

Teran-Victory was right. People around the world share the desire to "get away from it all"—now and then. And the world is full of places to do that.

# CHAPTER 10

# Commerce Is the World's Common Language

The streets are the shopping malls in many of the world's
great cities, like Seoul, Korea's Itaewon. There, people
bargain, barter, and banter all night long.
Photo: Callie Shell, *Nashville Tennessean*

WHEN Evelyn Lewis wasn't busy watching son Carl haul in gold at the 1988 Summer Olympics, she was taking part in an event herself—bargain-hunting.

Hurdler Edwin Moses' mom, Gladys, did the same thing. She said she lost control buying gifts for her grandchildren.

Evelyn Lewis put it this way: "I went crazy buying silk blouses."

Both went shopping at Itaewon— Seoul, South Korea's frenzied district of stores and discos. A shopper's paradise.

Bargaining, bartering, and bantering are part of everyday life around the world. We all hold commerce in common. From Korea to Hong Kong. From Singapore to San Jose. From Paris to Perth. From capitalism to communism. But just how and where it takes place, plus the wide range of goods sold, are excellent examples of the globe's rich diversity.

For some, pressing for the best deal is recreation. For others, it's part of the ongoing struggle to make ends meet. And for still others, it's business. Serious business. Regardless, when buying and selling take place, life almost always takes on a keen edge. No matter the culture or country.

Seoul's Itaewon is a good example. It was easily one of the most electrifying places we visited. Walk down the main street:

• You hear U.S. pop music blaring out.

• You listen to a mix of languages—Korean, French, lots of English. Many others.

• You witness an endless parade of people.

It's a social event. A place to see and be seen. A bit like the Atlantic City boardwalks. But above all, Itaewon is for the shop-till-you-drop marathon.

Shoppers and shopkeepers haggle. And haggle some more. And then some more.

Tough-talking touts seemingly leap from the shadows offering custom-made $150 suits, $120 leather bomber jackets, $10 dress shirts. There are amethyst pins, jade pendants, angora sweaters.

"More than anything else, it's fun," said Mike Ellis, a Sarasota, Florida, car dealer. "If you get taken, it's your own fault."

In Itaewon, what you see is what you get. But not everything you get is always what you thought you were seeing. Counterfeits are plentiful. There are fake Gucci purses. Fake Reebok shoes. Fake Adidas scarves. Fake Louis Vuitton handbags.

Unless you have a trained eye, you can't tell the difference.

"You open the inside of a bag and look at the lining," said Joyce Tarter from Chico, California. She opened a "Louis Vuitton" lined with vinyl.

"Forget it!" she exclaimed and walked away.

Like the Kenny Rogers song says, "You've got to know when to fold 'em, know when to hold 'em."

That's what haggling is all about—no matter which country you're in. It was the same on the other side of the world in

Sweden. Only there it all took place without a word being spoken.

The place: A market at the harbor of Gothenburg, Sweden's second-largest city and its gateway to the North Sea.

The event: A daily silent auction.

The product: Fish.

The auction begins in the early morning hours as hundreds of people gather around boxes and boxes of iced, freshly caught fish.

While one man with a clipboard recites prices in a sing-song voice, those around him make all kinds of gestures to get his attention. They twitch their eyebrows. Fiddle with their ears. Roll and blink their eyes. Open and close their mouths.

Nobody yells or raises his hands. Some, however, do make noises like barking seals or rumbling trucks.

It's all done to bid on fish.

"Sometimes its hard to remember where you are—a fish market or a zoo," said auctioneer and accountant Bert Larsson.

But rules are rules.

"The only time you use your hands or yell out a bid is when you're bidding in two auctions at the same time," said Iris Tobernston, who at sixty-eight has been buying fish at the Gothenburg fish auction for nearly half a century.

She uses her eyes.

The day JetCapade visited, some sixty-six thousand pounds of cod, mackerel, eel, flounder, ponfret, and other kinds of fish and crustaceans were on the block. Brought in by large and small fishing boats. Unloaded right there by the crews.

Larsson and three other auctioneers face anywhere from three hundred to eight hundred buyers every day. But sometimes there are more tourists than buyers in the crowd.

How to tell them apart?

"After you've been here awhile, you get to know the buyers, what they want to buy, and who has the money," explained Lars Erlandsson, at twenty-eight the youngest of the four auctioneers.

The whole thing is fun for tourists. But the silence can lead to mistakes, and mistakes have been made during the auction's seventy-nine-year history:

• Sometimes buyers from the same company bid against each other. Reason: They can't hear the bids come in.

• Other buyers mistakenly think they have won a bid. Reason: They haven't noticed the bid was won by a buyer sitting behind them.

The bidding is complete when the auctioneer thumps a pencil against his clipboard.

The fish auction began in 1910 and the biggest transactions took place in 1943, when for three days and three nights, buyers and auctioneers worked through 630,000 pounds of fish.

"There are fewer fish available now," Tobernston said. "But they are worth more. Prices are higher and more people are eating fish."

It's the same the world over. Every day. Buyers and sellers of all cultures wheeling and dealing for the right price. In the streets—the world's original shopping malls. In artisans' tiny back-street shops. In specialized markets. In the desert. Buying and selling is a worldwide connective tissue that links people to people and nations to nations.

———

### Buying a Camel Is Like Buying a Car

———

In the USA, an advertising slogan suggests some people will walk a mile for a Camel.

In Egypt, they will walk for forty days to sell one.

The day we visited the old, crumbling Imbaba district of Cairo, it was market day. Ill-humored camels stood in unruly rows, leashed to heavy cables draped across a dusty open field.

We met Abdel Nafee Batlan, a camel dealer. He deals in hundreds of them every month—either buying or reselling or acting as middleman.

"This one tried to bite," Batlan, forty, said with a laugh as he pointed out one of the camels. The camel, because of its bad habits, was tied by the nose to its leash.

Thick-chested Egyptian camels stood haughtily to one side of the field—not far from Batlan's green-painted office. They were work camels, used to haul everything from vegetables to wood to tourists.

In the center of the field stood slender camels from Sudan, the country just south of Egypt.

"They are for food, for eating," Batlan said. "Camel meat isn't bad. You cook it like beef."

And compared to beef and goat, camel meat is cheaper. Low-grade beef costs about $1.60 a pound. Goat meat goes for $1.52 a pound. Camel costs around $1 a pound.

Sudanese tribesmen bring their camels to Cairo in caravans from the south.

"We call this the walk of the forty days," Batlan said. That's how long it takes to journey from Sudan to the Imbaba market.

When Batlan gets ready to make a deal, he sizes up each camel, looking for injuries, old scars, and general appearance.

"The rule of thumb when buying a camel is to determine how many kilos it weighs," Batlan explained. (A kilo equals 2.2 pounds.)

The approximate retail price: five Egyptian pounds for each kilo.

Nearby, a potential buyer argued over two camels. He offered 1,600 Egyptian pounds for both. The Sudanese wanted 1,650 pounds. There was much shouting. They looked ready to fight.

"They are just bargaining," Batlan said, laughing again. "It's like buying a car."

The buyer gave in, agreeing to 1,650 pounds. The men shook hands to seal the deal. That was it. No contract, no warranty.

**These Sandals Have a Literary Sole**

Some people say there is poetry in the way Athenian Stavros Melissinos makes sandals.

"Making shoes *is* poetry," he told us, holding court behind a shoemaker's bench piled high with books, papers, and scraps of leather. "Making shoes and writing poetry, they go together, don't you know?"

That's true in Melissinos' case. He is a poet and a sandalmaker.

The poetry and plays Melissinos writes in his spare time.

The shoes Melissinos makes to earn a living. Learned the trade from his father.

In a crowded shop adjacent to Athens' Monastiriki Square, a colorful jumble of a flea market near the heart of the Greek capital, Melissinos and five employees make and sell sandals. Produce about ten thousand pairs a year.

And not just any sandals.

Though they cost no more than twenty drachmas, celebrities the world over have been among his clients.

At one time or another, Sophia Loren, Rudolf Nureyev, Jacqueline Onassis, the Beatles, Anthony Quinn, and George (*The A-Team*) Peppard have worn Melissinos' rubber-soled sandals. But most of his clients are tourists—U.S. tourists.

Melissinos, who learned English translating the works of Edgar Allan Poe into Greek, began writing poems and essays at the age of twelve.

Melissinos' sandals are on display in the store. His books are not. But he will produce them on request, and with a little urging he might even give a reading—while you're trying a pair of sandals.

***Singapore Got Street Vendors off Streets***

Until twenty years ago, a sea of street vendors flooded the sidewalks of Singapore, selling everything from fresh fruit to costume jewelry and plates of dim sum.

That changed in 1968. That's the year Singapore authorities decided that multitudes of street vendors were not only unsightly but unsanitary.

"Many of them used the same pail of water to wash plates and utensils—if they were washed at all," said one government official, who preferred to remain anonymous. "The unscrupulous ones would cheat customers and throw waste on roadsides and into sewers, which in turn contributed to the pollution of the Singapore River."

Result: All of Singapore's street vendors, or hawkers, were ordered off the streets and into neat, sanitary, government-controlled hawker centers.

Now there are 184 of these centers. They house the stalls of more than 25,000 of the former street vendors.

They do what they used to do before on the streets: sell everything from food to watches to the latest in electronics gadgets to counterfeit designer cloth.

But the shouting has stopped. The noise has stopped—except for USA pop music coming out of unseen loudspeakers.

It's now subdued. Improved. Sanitized. Functional. Efficient. Like most other things in Singapore.

But customers and many—but by no means all—hawkers seem satisfied with the arrangement.

"It's much better than being on the streets," said Low Kum Swee, forty-three, pointing to a rain-drenched street outside the Chinatown Hawkers' Center. "I'm not in the rain. You're not in the rain. I have electricity. I have a place for you to sit and a place to roast my ducks."

Food is a big item among the hawkers' products—and a popular one among locals and visitors alike.

Low, for example, owns the Xing Ming Barbecue stand, where rows of freshly cooked pork and smoked ducks, heads still on, are proudly displayed. His stand is flanked by two others. One sells prepared fish dishes. The other, fried noodle dishes.

"It's like fast food, only much, much better," Low said.

In another part of Singapore, at Sim Lin Square, Lee Ong Chun, forty-five, manages thirty food stalls.

"We have all kinds of food here—Chinese, Muslim, Korean, and Indonesian," Lee said. "But most of it is Chinese, although we also have Western food, like hot dogs and hamburgers, which are becoming more and more popular in Singapore."

Low, who sells Chinese food at about $1 a plate, is convinced things couldn't be better—even though he has to pay a monthly rent of $100.

"I worked on the streets of Singapore for fifteen years before moving into this center," he told us. "What I have to pay to be here is worth it."

Not every hawker agrees. A number of them still believe there's more money on the streets—even at the risk of running afoul of Singapore's strict cops.

The number of hawkers returning illegally to the streets seems to be growing—if the number of fines are any indication. Inspectors issued 12,738 tickets in 1985. It was 16,093 in 1986. And 17,290 in 1987.

Fines range from $500 to $2,000—and up to three years in jail for repeat offenders.

It's become a cat-and-mouse game between the cops and the hawkers. The latter use children and old folks as lookouts. Many use pocket telephone pagers to be warned of approaching officers.

Once warned, the unlicensed vendor quickly packs everything away. Or gives items away to passers-by—free of charge.

That's when you really can't beat the price.

***Bargaining Is Reborn in China***

Flea markets and swap meets are nothing new in the USA. They liven up weekends. Make buyers and sellers happy. Let old stuff find a new home.

Bargaining habits were all but lost in China under the weight of communism. But they are slowly coming back, especially in the "free markets." The markets are symbols of China's blossoming consumerism and budding capitalism.

The free markets are an excellent place to get a sense of the new China—and the new Chinese. That's what we did in Beijing, Guangzhou, and Shenzen.

We met Chen Muxung, eighteen, in Guangzhou. A recent high school graduate. He was running a cassette music business at the Liwan District free market.

His inventory: about six hundred cassettes and one snazzy cassette player.

By USA standards, the prices were cheap: $1.35 to $2 for a cassette.

Also, by USA standards, Chen's profit is not much. About a quarter per tape. He sells as many as forty per day. About 10 bucks worth.

Other examples of China's new commercialism.

• In Shenzen, one of China's booming special economic zones, people from nearby Hong Kong—as adept at wheeling and dealing as anybody in the world—have discovered the free markets. They make day trips and often bring back boats full of bargains. One man claimed he bought a fighting bird for the equivalent of $40. It sells for $2,000 in Hong Kong.

• In Beijing, bargaining is a hit-or-miss proposition. Some free-market dealers, used to government controls, set one price and don't budge. Others—the quick learners—are beginning to appreciate the art of bargaining and becoming quite good at it.

Foreign visitors should compare before shopping. Government stores may sound and feel safer, but there are bargains to be had at the free markets. An $8 kite bought at one of the government's Friendship stores turned out to cost less than half that on the street.

Even if you buy nothing, the free markets are worth touring just for the gawking. They are brimming with Chinese life and goods:

• There are painters, calligraphers, and puppetmakers. Toy and craft handiworkers.

• There are chickens, shrimp, eels, ducks, and frogs.

• There are birds and goldfish, so beloved by the Chinese.

It's buying and selling. It's China up close.

———

### *"The Stomach of Europe"*

———

No matter where or what you eat in Paris, the fare probably came from Paris' Rungis Market.

It's known there as the "Stomach of Europe."

"This is one of the few markets in the world where a buyer can truly find everything under one roof," said Henry Gerant, sixty-three. He's a farmer whose family has been bringing produce to Rungis for five generations.

Rungis is a hundred-fifty-year-old, seven-hundred-acre market located near Orly International Airport. It's where quality reigns supreme. And, so it seems, does chaos.

Outside the nearly endless rows of football field-sized buildings, massive traffic jams are created by honking cars and huge trucks. And people are continuously scurrying between the vehicles and from one building to another.

But that's orderly compared to the mayhem inside.

There are buyers everywhere:

• Independent buyers

• Buyers for restaurants—the big-name places and the small, side-street bistros

• Buyers for food exporters; for supermarket chains; for small grocers

• Buyers riding motorbikes or bicycles down aisles laden with food from all over the world

• Buyers running, dodging dollies filled with yet more food
And there is food everywhere:

• Meat, fish, cheese, all housed in separate buildings

• Fruits and vegetables—asparagus from France and Israel; apples from New Zealand and South Africa; grapefruit from the USA; peaches and oranges from Spain; beans and mushrooms from France, Africa, and Brazil

Quality comes first. Prices come second.

"People sell things at whatever prices they think they can get," said Sarah Flamini, twenty-six, fruit and vegetable buyer for Djen Maurice, one of 280 companies located at Rungis.

Example: A box of morels or chanterelles, two types of rare mushrooms, sold for $200 a box when we visited.

"Competition here is outrageous," echoed Jean-Claude Lassille, forty-five, who buys fish, meat, fruit, and vegetables for eight Parisian restaurants. "It can lead to fistfights because everyone wants the best."

———

**You Can Find Anything in Hong Kong**

———

So many bargains. So little time.

That's how many visitors feel upon landing in this British-held, duty-free port on China's south coast.

Credit cards at the ready, foreign shoppers walk out of their hotels in Hong Kong into what is practically one gigantic open-air shopping mall. And it's all on the streets.

Helen Giss has raised shopping in Hong Kong to an art form—and a business.

The Louisiana native knows that mixed feeling of anticipation and frustration that overwhelms many foreign shoppers in a hurry.

"I think that's why my business is so successful," she told us. "Tourists have stacks of shopping information from friends and from articles. They are overwhelmed."

So she started Asian Cajun to help guide tourists and foreign shoppers through the merchandise maze that is the streets of Hong Kong.

It's not cheap—$40 an hour with a three-hour minimum. But she figures that with her help, shoppers might save that much—or more—on bargains.

Always haggle, she advises. Offer half of what the merchant wants.

With that in mind, you can buy anything on the streets of Hong Kong, she said. "Anything."

But to do it right, she recommends:
• Know what you want.
• Know the prices at home.
• Check out friends' recommendations carefully.

What are good buys in Hong Kong?

Experts—and those who think they are—agree that it's almost everything. But outstanding are leather goods, linens, clothes by local designers, pearls, gold jewelry, optics, antiques, ivory, and computer software.

But be wary of cameras and electronics, unless they're new. And even then, they're not much of a bargain if compared to the USA.

Then there are "designer" clothing, "designer" jewelry, and "designer" watches. Cartier and Rolex—but probably mostly counterfeit.

"I can get you a fake Rolex for thirty-one dollars," Giss said.

Whatever the product, Hong Kong probably has it on its streets. And the streets never sleep. A shopper's delight.

*A Place Where*
*Electronic*
*Variety Is*
*Electrifying*

In Tokyo, Akihabara is an electronics addict's idea of heaven.

They have everything there—from digital audio tape (DAT) players to automatic bread makers.

Akihabara is a noisy Tokyo district. It's home to at least two hundred shops—big and small—crammed with every imaginable Japanese electronic appliance.

Pop music pounds from stereo speakers. Flashing red, blue, and orange lights beckon shoppers. Prices are marked, but bargaining is welcome.

"Shoppers come for video cameras, video recordings and the new DAT players," said Mamoro Ogura, forty-seven, manager of the Saeki Musen store in Akihabara.

DAT technology, capable of faithfully copying other digital products like compact discs, is still new to the USA. And the USA music industry wants to restrict imports or put anticopy chips into discs.

But USA shoppers who go to Akihabara are undaunted. They buy DAT players—even though they cost as much as $1,100 each.

There's another attraction at Akihabara. It's the sheer variety of electronics products available—more than in many comparable stores in the USA.

"For example, there might be just ten different models of a Japanese-manufactured cassette player sold in the USA," Ogura said. "Here in Akihabara, we can find fifty models."

There are also, among many other things, mini-satellite dishes for the well-heeled television viewer (about $1,400, installation included). And the automatic bread makers.

The latter is among the latest in Japanese electronics gadgetry to hit the USA. The cube-shaped units knead the bread, let it rise, and then bake it.

Takao Kawauchi, fifty, has eight models in his store.

But like many other gadgets, the bread maker is already

on its way to obsolescence in Japan. They're becoming as stale as old bread.

"At the beginning, we sold fifty to sixty units a month," Kawauchi said. "Now we sell fifteen units a month. Products here can quickly become obsolete."

---

### The Street Is World's "Marketplace"

Much of the world's marketplace is not the shopping mall or the department store or even the small back-street shop. It's the street. That's the showroom and sales floor for many of the goods and services sold. That's the home and workplace for many of the world's merchants.

We met hundreds of examples:

• Walter Baumann, thirty-three. He sells fruits and vegetables twice a week at a street market in Bern, Switzerland's central square. Baumann has a farm near the small Bernese community of Kirchdorf. His grandfather started the business forty years ago and, he told us, "You'd be amazed how many people buy my goods because they like natural food, even though our stuff is about fifteen to twenty percent more expensive."

• Agnes Manas, thirty-five. She has a vegetable and fruit stand in Nice's main street market, just one block from the French Riviera. We talked to her early one Sunday morning while she was busy selling carrots, tomatoes, asparagus, apples, pineapples, and other fruits and vegetables. "Ever since the big supermarkets opened, business for us hasn't been too good, except on Sundays when the supermarkets and stores are closed," she said.

• Sandra de la Bevy de la Faverges, twenty-one, and her father, Antoine, sixty-three. They own a news stand on Nice's Avenue Jean Medecin. He complained about teen-age street crime and said he's ready to defend his business. To prove it, he pulled a switchblade and a handgun out of a drawer and proudly showed them off. "I almost had to use one of these recently," he said.

• Fatma Hassan, about fifty. She was busy selling newspapers at a Cairo marketplace. "My husband died and I have to sell to feed my boy and girl," she told us.

• Nelson de Souza Neves, forty. He sells oranges on the streets of Rio de Janeiro. "We make enough money to live off of, but not that much," he said.

• Dario Jorge Montes, twelve. He's a precocious, talkative fifth grader who watches and washes cars on the streets just two blocks from the beach in Mar del Plata, a popular Argentine summer resort two hundred fifty miles southeast of Buenos Aires.

He likes math and swimming and soccer—and wants to make lots of money someday working with computers. But meanwhile, the streets are his office and competition is tough.

"I don't have time to go to the beach because I'm always working and you really have to watch out around here," he told us. Then, pointing at a boy about his age watching him from about half a block away, he said: "You see that guy over there? He stole ten Australes [then about $1.80] from me this morning."

• Pupua Kumar Harovar, twelve. He shines shoes in one of the busiest shopping areas in the old part of Delhi, India. He charges 30 cents—and is good at what he does. He's been shining shoes in Delhi's Connaught Place area for four years. But, he told us, "this is not what I plan to do much longer. Someday I would like to be a gold trader.

Each is a merchant in the world's most enduring marketplace—the street.

***Commerce—
A Global
Language***

In Gothenburg, Sweden, people buy and sell fish without saying a word.

In Seoul, South Korea, people buy and sell just about everything with high-pitched haggling in a multitude of tongues.

These two examples demonstrate how diverse commerce is around the world. And, at the same time, how much it is the same. No matter what language is being spoken, no matter what product is being sold, bantering, bartering, and bargaining are global concepts.

A buyer and a seller speaking two different languages still manage to communicate. There's a meeting of the minds when the price is right.

# CHAPTER 11

# People Want to Make a Difference

Risk takers. Organizers. Doers. Achievers, like British
entrepreneur Richard Branson of Virgin Atlantic Airways,
have stepped out on a limb and made millions—
or found happiness.
Photo: Carol Halebian

OM Parkash Yadav would win an Horatio Alger award if he lived in the USA. He's owner of a New Delhi taxi business. Takes home $230 a month. Not many years ago, he was washing cars for four cents each.

O.P.—that's short for Om Parkash—started out in poverty in Kaliawas, a dusty village of fifteen hundred people that's thirty-one miles from New Delhi. It's nothing but a cluster of mud, cement, and brick houses, a place where the electricity only comes on at night and the water only comes from a communal tap. His is a classic rags-to-riches story.

"I was a very poor boy with no education," O.P. told us in good English—a language he's never studied but now speaks fluently with verve.

O.P., thirty-two, is the oldest of six sons. Started working on his father's twenty-five-acre farm so long ago he can't remember exactly how old he was. Quit school after the fifth grade. Then left for New Delhi because there were no schools, jobs, or opportunities left in Kaliawas.

"I washed cars for half a rupee [0.04 U.S. cents at prevailing rates]. At night I went with the taxi people and helped them. Washing their taxis and getting them tea," O.P. recalled as he wound his way through the Delhi traffic.

In 1972 he started driving for a tour company. Two years later, he got a 16 percent loan and bought a cab.

O.P.'s business took off when he landed a spot in the taxi stand at one of Delhi's most luxurious hotels—the Maurya Sheraton. A privilege that costs him $11 a month.

By mid-1988, O.P. owned three taxis, planned to buy a fourth, and controlled a 25 percent share in a taxi stand near the U.S. Embassy in Delhi's affluent diplomatic enclave.

"I'm at the top," O.P. told us with pride. A pride shared by his father, Shrichand Yadav, sixty, who has no plans to leave his farm or his village. "Who even needs to ask? Of course I'm proud of him."

A lot of O.P.'s earnings make it back to Kaliawas, where his parents, brothers, nieces, and nephews live in two whitewashed stone houses.

The family has a radio and a TV set—thanks to O.P. He's also bought his father a tractor, and two younger brothers drive his other two taxis. In fact, nine of the hotel's forty taxis are driven by O.P.'s relatives.

"My family is not helping me. I help my family," O.P. said. "If I hadn't helped, they'd be like other farmers. If I do well, my brother also does well. If we join together we're more successful."

O.P.'s success story was only one of many we came across. Stories of people determined to succeed—no matter what the obstacles. People with every reason to give up. But people who won't. And don't.

Why? Because they all share an enduring desire to make it. They have a tireless drive to improve their lives and, very often, the lives of those around them.

Richard Branson was another good example. He's the man

the British press dubbed "Prime Minister Margaret Thatcher's favorite entrepreneur."

Branson dropped out of school at fifteen. Started his first business venture at age eighteen. And by the time we met him, he was thirty-seven and worth half a billion dollars—with a home in London and another in Oxford.

His growing international empire—the Virgin Group—includes an airline called Virgin Atlantic, record stores, hotels, a recording company, a publishing company, satellite broadcasting stations, and a condom factory that uses the brand name Mates.

He's also the business brains behind Boy George & the Culture Club, Phil Collins, and the Sex Pistols.

Branson directs it all from an old wooden houseboat, the *Duende* (Spanish for "ghost"), anchored in the Regent Canal in London's Paddington section.

"Obviously I'm an entrepreneur, and there haven't been that many to come out of Britain, mainly because up until some ten years ago, entrepreneurs were frowned upon. For example, there's never been an entrepreneur—ever—to come out of Oxford and Cambridge," Branson told us.

Apparently British youth were in the mood for a big-time entrepreneur. A 1988 poll rated Branson, who prefers open-neck shirts, colorful sweaters, and corduroy slacks, the third most popular person—behind Prince Charles and the Pope.

Branson stressed that he sees himself as a person who tries to use his wealth with "a social conscience. I'm not flaunting my wealth too much . . . and when you look back at your life when you're sixty-five or seventy years old and you realize you've used your wealth constructively, you will have lived a happier life."

In early 1988, Branson became the first West European to become a member of the Intourist board, the official Soviet tourist agency. For starters, that means Virgin Atlantic will be flying once a week from London to Moscow. Branson also is trying to swing a $300 million condoms-for-oil deal. He thinks the Soviets might be interested because they "don't have real condoms."

But Branson's main target is the USA. Virgin Atlantic already flies from London to Newark and Miami and Boston. He will add a New York–to–Los Angeles leg in 1989. But he would like to expand some of his other ventures in the USA.

Why? Because he sees opportunity.

"We have been profitable in every other country of the world where we have operated [seventeen at last count], but America is the most expensive market to crack and we wanted to wait until we were strong enough. And now we are," he said.

And there were others. Many ambitious others. People who want to make a mark:

• Serena Ng was only eighteen when we met her. But she already knew exactly what she wanted: to have her own boutique for women in Singapore.

"I'm going to work and build my career," Serena said. "I just want to be rich enough to live."

Ng is a sales clerk at Singapore's Premptem Department Store during the day. At night, she takes art and design classes to help her career.

• Lavilla Pitts, forty-three, used to be a surgical nurse in Madison, Wisconsin. Then she and husband Fred Pitts, a sixty-year-old former neurosurgeon, bade farewell to the cold Midwest and went to tropical Costa Rica. Today she owns a flourishing fashion design business in San Jose.

• Chun Byung-tak owns a shop in Seoul called The First Flower Garden. "I think I will be very successful because more and more people have been buying flowers," he told us. "The level of Korea's standard of living is rising, and so Koreans have more and more time for leisure things—like flowers."

• Neil Clapperton, thirty, is co-owner of Caddenheads Whisky Shop in Edinburgh. He took over the store in 1987, giving up his earlier career as a window-dresser. "The United Kingdom is a better and better place for people to go into business for themselves," he said.

• Bobby Bernini, forty-two, is the manager of Flanagan's, a fish & chips restaurant—looking and feeling as British as can be. Located on Baker Street in London's City of Westminster. USA-style fast food places are mushrooming all over London and there's a McDonald's just a few doors down from Flanagan's. "Places like this are still doing well," Bernini told us. "This proves that good restaurants will always be around."

And, it seems, so will enterprising people seeking success. The dream to make a mark is alive around the world. It's the dream that transcends cultural, economic, and political boundaries.

### *Making a Fortune Cookie Fortune*

It may be duck soup selling Big Macs and Kentucky Fried Chicken to the Chinese in Hong Kong, but try peddling fortune cookies. Folks there don't know what to do with them.

But Shanghai-born entrepreneur Nancy Hsu-Anderson, forty-one, is changing all that. She began importing Los Angeles–made fortune cookies to Hong Kong in May 1987. Got the idea from her American journalist-husband Paul eight years ago. He discovered that meals in Hong Kong don't end with a fortune cookie.

Based on Hsu-Anderson's research, fortune cookies are a Chinese-American invention. The mass emigration of Chinese workers who came to the USA in the early twentieth century resulted in an explosion of Chinese restaurants. Hsu-Anderson believes fortune cookies were a gimmick the Chinese concocted to attract more customers.

Hsu-Anderson's idea became a reality following a chance encounter with the marketing manager of Umeya, a Japanese-American company and the largest fortune-cookie maker on the West Coast. The meeting ended with a contract to ship cookies to Hong Kong by plane.

"A handshake did it all," Hsu-Anderson said.

The first shipment to her Dragon Heart Company in Hong Kong totaled seventy cartons—twenty-eight hundred cookies.

Price to Hong Kong's customers? About 17 cents each.

The marketing challenge? Explaining to Hong Kong gourmet deli owners what the cookies were and then convincing them that tourists and "chompies" would love them.

"Chompies" is Hsu-Anderson's word for young Hong Kong Chinese professionals who studied in the USA and have eaten at USA Chinese restaurants.

"Chompies are always eating and know about fortune cookies," she said. So "chompies" were the logical market. "Serving a fortune cookie to dinner guests would be stylish and would communicate that they had been to the United States," she reasoned.

So far, it has worked. The delis are selling out and restocking.

Next goal: Sell a hundred thousand cookies in a year. She's now aiming for upscale hotels and private clubs serving Chinese food. Hsu-Anderson thinks it's time the fortune cookie replaced the piece of chocolate many hotels leave on pillows at night.

Chinese restaurants will be the biggest challenge.

"There is no tradition among Chinese here for fortune cookies. The people here wouldn't know how to treat them. They'd be very skeptical. They would ask, what do I do with the paper?

"And they couldn't grasp buying more than one and everyone opening them up together and sharing their messages. You'd have to explain all this, and that of course would spoil the fun," she said.

Chinese traditionally have gone to the temple whenever they've wanted their fortunes told. To get them to accept good fortune baked in a cookie is a challenge Hsu-Anderson welcomes.

"I'm proud to be Shanghainese," she said. "That's where the spirit of entrepreneurs is strong."

***He's a Pioneer
on Spanish-
Language TV***

Raul Velasco is a modern Mexican success story. A product of the electronic age. He rose from provincial obscurity to hemispheric fame in full view of the public—on television.

In the early 1970s Velasco was a reporter for a local newspaper in Mexico writing about television show business.

Today, Velasco is a household word throughout Latin America and in many parts of the USA.

This is because Velasco, fifty-five, has for the past eighteen years been the host of Latin America's most popular television variety show. What Ed Sullivan used to do on USA television every Sunday in the fifties and sixties.

Called *Siempre en Domingo* (Always on Sunday), this Mexico-based three-and-a-half-hour show attracts more than two hundred million viewers in Latin America and the USA every Sunday.

"Many people have talked to me and written to me and said that even if they don't understand what I'm saying, they consider my show to be another musical option—an alternative, if you will," he told us in his Mexico City office.

"Most Anglo music is either country or rock, but we offer a different kind of music and singers like Julio Iglesias [from Spain but now living in southern Florida] and El Puma [the nickname of Venezuelan pop singer José Luis Rodriguez]."

But well-known U.S. artists have also been on his show: Tina Turner, Michael Jackson, and Whitney Houston.

Given the growing popularity of his show among USA viewers, Velasco considers himself sort of the pioneer of Spanish-language television in the USA.

"I suppose I have been fortunate enough to be just that. My program has been able to contribute to popularizing Spanish-language television" in the USA, Velasco said.

### His Little Newspaper Is a Worldwide Institution

Costa Rica's Richard Dyer has been a journalist for almost six decades. And much of that time has been devoted to the *Tico Times*—probably the best-known English-language newspaper in Central America.

Dyer started out as a reporter in the USA in 1931. Worked for the Associated Press, the Oakland *Post Enquirer,* and the San Francisco *Examiner.*

The San Jose–based *Tico Times* was not his idea. Local high school students came up with it. They thought it would be a good introduction to journalism before entering college journalism programs in the USA.

So Dyer and his wife, Betty, who had been a New York *Post* reporter, saw an opportunity—and launched their paper in 1951. Betty died in 1971.

Today, the *Times* is something of an institution. Its reputation—and its seven thousand circulation—go far beyond the West Virginia-sized country where it's based. Nearly half of the *Times'* subscribers live in the USA. "And we even have one subscriber in Kabul, Afghanistan," Dyer, seventy-six, told us in San Jose.

"People everywhere are interested in Costa Rica, in Central America, and the Caribbean. They just don't get that kind of coverage from other media," he said.

"We are like Central America's hometown newspaper," he proudly told us.

The idea—and the paper—have long since caught on. Dyer has made his mark.

*Modern Manager Makes Desert Fertile*

You don't usually think of farms and green pastures when it comes to Saudi Arabia. Oil and bone-dry deserts are more likely images.

That's what makes Saleh Showami special.

He's a farmer. Works land that produces wheat, barley, fodder, and vegetables. In Saudi Arabia.

When Showami wants to take a one-day once-over of the farm he operates in Haradh, in the eastern part of the oil-rich desert kingdom, it means a ninety-mile trip: That's because his thirteen thousand acres stretch sinuously for forty-five miles along an old riverbed that's seldom more than a mile wide. It all belongs to the Saudi government.

But Showami represents the kind of young, highly educated farmer-manager the Saudis hope will make the kingdom self-sufficient in food.

Based on Showami's success, the Saudis are well on their way. Showami has a productive three-thousand-head dairy herd. He also has sheep. And honeybees are next.

Showami comes from a rural family, and his father's farm is at the other end of Saudi Arabia. "When I tell him how many hectares we have, he can't believe it," Showami told us. (One hectare equals 2.47 acres.)

Showami is typical of the new breed of manager in Saudi Arabia. Like many of them, he studied in the USA. In Arizona and in Minnesota. Arizona he remembers as too hot. Minnesota as too cold.

But in Minnesota, the depth of the soil and the amount of rain impressed him. "The farmers just plant their seeds and leave them," he said.

It will never be that easy in Saudi Arabia. But that won't stop Showami.

Kevin Kilmartin, an Englishman, went to the Falkland Islands on holiday in 1976. And never left.

Today he owns and operates the Bluff Cove sheep farm in the Falklands—the British-controlled South Atlantic islands claimed by Argentina and the site of a bloody war between the two countries in 1982.

Kilmartin, thirty-eight, is a Londoner, as is his wife, Diane, a former nurse who joined him later. Their daughter, Claire, was born on the islands in 1986.

"This is home now," he told us during a visit to his sheep farm. "It wasn't planned that way, but it has worked out that way. And it's fine by us."

When Kilmartin arrived he owned neither land nor sheep.

Today he owns one of the "smaller" farms: thirty thousand acres stocked with three thousand sheep.

"We're now moving away from large absentee owners to smaller farms," he said. "My neighbor down the road has a hundred thousand sheep."

Kilmartin talked to us while he was busy folding fleece skillfully shorn off his sheep by three Falkland shearers—Peter Morrison, twenty-five, Lenny Ford, twenty-one, and Donald Betts, thirty-two.

Each fleece weighs about three kilos (6.6 pounds). The current price in the United Kingdom is about $4.75 per kilo. That would mean that Kilmartin's income is about $40,000—before taxes, expenses, and wages.

"If you're summing it all up, you'll see why many are quitting this business," he said. But Kilmartin is staying in the sheep business.

The neighbor down the road that Kilmartin spoke of is the Falkland Islands Company. FIC owns about 40 percent of the islands' land and nearly one half of the sheep. It is a subsidiary of Coalite, a British coal and shipping conglomerate.

For most of the islands' modern history, FIC has been economic power in the Falklands.

But since the 1982 war, FIC has sold off fifty-acre plots along the main road to people like Kilmartin. He's confident—and determined—that smaller, more efficient ranchers will become the norm. Motorbike herding is one example of this new efficiency.

"We used to shepherd them with dogs and horses. Now we use dogs and motorbikes," Kilmartin said.

"We've moved from twenty big farms to seventy smaller ones since the war," said Kilmartin, who lost several hundred sheep to Argentine soldiers camped in nearby hills who slaughtered and ate them.

There are nearly seven hundred thousand sheep on the Falkland Islands and less than two thousand people. Needless to say, that makes wool king in the Falklands.

Even so, the Falklands will never become one of the world's major world producers. Australia, which is No. 1, has 150 million sheep.

"We're still one of the smallest producers in the world," Kilmartin said. But he didn't seem discouraged.

———

### Boomerang Business Is Booming

———

Sam Blight thought boomerangs had an image problem, so he set out to fix it. And make a little money at the same time.

Blight, thirty-three, from the Western Australian town of Nedlands, was upset about boomerangs being regarded as nothing more than a souvenir—"a joke, in the very land where they were invented.

"It's no wonder," he told us. "They've been so poorly made that most people's experience with them has been negative: the things either break or don't work, or both."

Blight's interest in boomerangs and other things that fly is not recent. He's been fascinated with them since he was a child. When he was ten, he tried to fly—from the roof of his father's garage with the help of cardboard wings. He crashed. But he didn't lose interest.

Countless model airplanes, crudely made birds, and boomerangs later, he figured he was ready. He started making boomerangs—not for decoration but for flying. Just like the Aborigines intended when they started it all.

"You'd be surprised how few Australians have ever seen a boomerang fly," he said. But then he added a positive note: "That's changing."

In 1980, Blight and his partner, Maureen Boland, thirty-seven, set out to make sure it changed. That's when they borrowed $100 and bought the best piece of wood they could find. Blight then crafted some boomerangs on his brother's back porch and Rangs Aerodynamic Sports Boomerangs was launched.

Boland sold the boomerangs at prices ranging from $25 to $50.

"We discovered that our market was very upscale . . . the junky souvenir shops just didn't want them," she said.

Since then, Rangs has grown into a company that:
- Employs eighteen workers
- Grosses more than $300,000
- Produces about sixty thousand homemade boomerangs a year; of these, about 20 percent are shipped to the USA to be sold in catalog and specialty stores

"The business has doubled every year," said Boland, who moved to Western Australia from Alexandria, Virginia, when she was seventeen.

"It's like riding a bucking bronco."

**"McFurrier" Is
Pleased with
His Title**

Kim Young-Do doesn't mind being called "McFurrier." And he doesn't resent wisecracks about "fast fur."

In fact, Kim chuckles all the way to the company cash register—and the bank—at his competitors' caustic comments about his techniques.

His company, Jindo Corporation, located in an industrial park outside Seoul, is the world's largest manufacturer of fur coats—$264 million worth in 1987.

And Kim is out to wrap the world's women in fox and mink.

Kim told us he offers a good product at reasonable prices. In that USA corporate tradition.

"Our idea is that it's our duty to provide very good quality for garments at reasonable prices," said Kim, the forty-five-year old president of the company.

His four brothers also hold executive positions in Jindo.

Kim's prime customers are first-time fur owners—especially for mink.

"Young people also like it and young ladies can afford it," he told us. "For a long time it was very prestigious and expensive. But a two-thousand-dollar mink coat is very popular and office girls can afford it."

Kim admits that his company takes a lot of heat from environmentalists and animal rights activists in Europe and the USA. But he doesn't seem overly worried about it. After all, he said, people also wear shoes, "and how can we make leather shoes without killing cows?"

Kim's "McFurrier" factory has become a favorite stopping point for tour buses with shoppers. Buyers can get a bigger selection there.

Kim counts on success breeding success. Plans to open twenty-five new stores in the near future. He already operates forty-four outlets—eleven in the USA, the others in Korea, Hong Kong, West Germany, and Great Britain.

His goal: "Global ten."

Explained his assistant, U.S. citizen Helen Li: "Of all the women in the world who wear furs, we want one in every ten to be wearing a Jindo fur."

**Watchmaking
Is His Dream
Come True**

Dominique Loiseau is a watchmaker. A Swiss watchmaker, to be precise.

From his workshop window in the Swiss city of Neuchâtel, Loiseau, thirty-nine, looks over the foothills of the Alps. And ponders.

"Everything is counted in time—life, death, happiness, and tears—there's never enough time. But timepieces, clocks, watches help man feel as if he has captured a piece of it. That helps people to dream," he said.

In 1984, Loiseau put his money where his skill is and captured a piece of that dream. That's when he created the Rose of Time—one of the world's most expensive clocks.

It was sold two years later to the Sultan of Brunei—one of the world's richest men.

Price: $1.5 million.

It took Loiseau ten thousand hours—the equivalent of 417 days—to make the Rose. He assembled each of its nine thousand pieces by hand. Including a golden rose of nine petals on top of the clock. The Rose opens and closes each half hour.

The clock is made of gold and encrusted with precious stones. It performs thirty-two functions, including keeping track of astrological changes over South America, New York, Bern, and Sydney, Australia. It also records the rising and setting of the sun and moon and the passage of days, months, and years. And, of course, the time of day.

To be sure, not every Loiseau timepiece has a million-dollar price tag. He makes about four or five watches a year—on request and entirely of gold.

Average price: $180,000.

"Loiseau is a genius," said Alain Bianchi, a spokesman for the Swiss Watchmakers Association. "He creates clocks for an old-fashioned reason—because he loves it. He's a complete artisan."

He is indeed more than just a watchmaker. He is by turns a goldsmith, jeweler, engraver, and technician.

"Craftsmen in other countries perfected various aspects of wristwatches," Loiseau told us. "The Swiss contributed precision."

But, precision or not, the Swiss watch industry fell on hard times beginning in the early 1970s when Japan and Hong Kong began mass marketing quartz and digital watches.

The Swiss are coming back, but probably will never beat the Japanese and Hong Kong in production. And they don't seem to care.

Reason: Switzerland never lost its spot as the world's top exporter of high-priced luxury watches—with the USA as its No. 1 market.

"When people see such watches, it makes them dream," Loiseau said.

———

***We Found Winners Around the World***

The dictionary defines an achievement as "something that has been accomplished successfully, especially by means of skill and perseverance."

The accomplishments of many people we met around the world fit that description.

They always were risk-takers. Organizers. Doers. Achievers.

And quite often, they were winners.

In a way, Lelah Santiago, twenty-seven, of Quezon City, near Manila, represented them all. No matter what their goals.

Santiago used to teach transport economics at the University of the Philippines in Manila. Now she owns Le San's Pastry Shop in the back of her home.

"I just got tired of teaching," she told us. "I was planning to start a business and it clicked."

And so it has for millions of others who have sought and found success in business.

# CHAPTER 12

# Crime Holds the World Hostage

Crime takes its toll around the world. But citizens and police
are fighting back. In 1985, more than 640 accused Mafia
members were herded into holding cells in Naples, Italy, and
guarded by 1,000 policemen until they could be tried.

Photo: Giansanti/Sygma

A ILTON Games da Silva, seventeen, of Rio de Janeiro, was on his way to work when we interviewed him. He couldn't talk long.

His occupation: Professional thief.

His target: Foreign tourists.

His income: $400 a day.

"It's easier than working," said this cocky crook. "This is a very easy job. And frankly, I'm the best there is."

Da Silva leads one of Rio's most notorious gangs. They've robbed hundreds of tourists. Fought with and reportedly killed dozens of rival gang members. Torched entire villages.

Da Silva—police later told us—is a wanted man.

We conducted our interview with da Silva behind a gas station. Across the street from a school. In mid-afternoon. When classes were letting out. So he could disappear into a group of students, if need be.

He was dressed like a well-to-do teen-ager. Clean. Handsome. Short hair. Perfect teeth. Fancy blue-flowered shirt. Fashionable jeans.

"If I look like a robber, the tourists will run from me before I approach them. So I have to buy—not steal—some nice clothes, comb my hair, look good," said da Silva, constantly on the lookout for police.

It took us nearly a week to track him down. A friend of his helped. Told da Silva it was safe: The interview wouldn't be pubished in Brazil.

But it was only after the interview that we learned more:

• Da Silva allegedly had fatally shot a tourist days earlier.

• He had gang members nearby watching us to make sure we weren't police.

• He had threatened to make his friend "pay" if anything happened to him because of the interview.

• He had given us a false name. Da Silva, his friend told us, was not this thief's real name.

Da Silva—proud as a peacock—told us his job is simple: "I use a revolver. The people don't do a thing except scream. They hand over rings, watches, bags." Rarely put up a fight.

He's one of millions making his life from crime. In all corners and countries of the world. Some work independently. Others are part of organized groups.

But all are lawbreakers. Terrifying other people. Forcing many to arm themselves—or stay indoors. Making them feel like a hostage.

Two examples:

• "After seven P.M., there is no one on the streets. We're scared to go out," said Jeeten Malhan, thirty-five, of New Delhi, India, who manages an aviation service company. "With all the crime and terrorism around, it's the innocent people getting hurt. One always fears something will happen."

• "I'm not afraid of lightning, wolves, or the night. Just man," said Damianos Gatsos, fifty-seven, a shepherd in Siderohori, Greece. "When one of them sneaks up on you, you'd better look out."

Crime is rampant—and on the rise—in many countries. A 1988 U.S. Department of Justice report on forty-one nations showed:

• Crime rates increased in Europe, Canada, Australia, and New Zealand between 1980 and 1984—the latest years for which figures are available—for everything except murder.

• Violent crime rates in the USA were four to nine times higher than those in Europe. That means more homicides, rapes, and robberies.

Other reports show:

• Brazil has the world's highest per capita murder rate: 104 registered homicides per 100,000 in 1983—or 370 a day, according to the *Guinness Book of World Records.*

• Crime in the Soviet Union—which has long been a secret—rose 17 percent in 1988, according to Soviet Interior Minister Vadim V. Bakatin. Attacks on police and street crime, up 40 percent. And police corruption is soaring, he said.

• Smuggling, embezzlement, bribery, swindling, and profiteering in China jumped 55 percent in 1986 to seventy-eight thousand cases, according to Zheng Tianxiang, president of the Supreme People's Court.

• Computer crime, piracy, and family violence are on the rise worldwide, according to the Seventh United Nations Congress on the Prevention of Crime and the Treatment of Offenders. More can be expected, the group said, as socioeconomic conditions worsen.

There are dozens of other examples of crime out of control.

But at least two countries boast of low crime rates: Saudi Arabia, which claims to have the lowest crime rate in the world, and Singapore. Both attribute their success to stiff penalties, swift justice.

Example: Two days before we arrived in Riyadh, Saudi Arabia, two men were beheaded: one for murder, the other for adultery.

Convicted thieves in Saudi Arabia pay their penalty by having their hands, arms, feet, or legs cut off. Those guilty of capital crimes are beheaded in public ceremonies. Each be-heading must be approved by the king.

Latest tallies: fifty-one executions in 1987; eleven in 1986; forty-four in 1985.

Singapore has its own standards of punishment.

"Crime is well under control here," said Chan Choo Giap of Singapore's Central Police Station.

No wonder. Spit on a sidewalk, pay $75. Litter in a public place, fork over $500.

Commit rape and you'll be cane-whipped—if a doctor says you're healthy enough—as soon as you begin your prison sentence. Example: Armed robbery calls for twenty-four strokes of the cane to the buttocks with enough force to break the skin.

Murder, kidnapping, and drug-selling mean certain death.

Fewer crimes are committed in Singapore on a per capita basis than in most countries. In the USA, 5,207 crimes were committed per 100,000 people in 1987, compared to 1,491 in Singapore.

Also aiding Singaporean police: "Most people will provide us with good information leading to the culprit's arrest," Giap said.

But crime is more than theft and murder:

• Prostitution—which some call the "victimless crime"—is nearly universal. JetCapade staff members were proposi-tioned in Nairobi, Seoul, Havana, Moscow, Manila, and Mexico City. Some requested payment in U.S. currency. Others wanted clothes, cigarettes, and perfumes made in the USA.

In Moscow, prostitutes sometimes wait outside your hotel rooms in the hallway until you return.

• Bribery is big. Especially in many African countries. One JetCapade reporter was forced to pay five Kenyan customs officials $100 each before he could leave the country.

• Illegal money conversion is rampant. As is the black market. Youths approached JetCapade staffers in Moscow ho-tels, parks, stores, and even in Red Square in front of Lenin's Tomb, rode hotel elevators with us to our floors, all the while trying to strike up a bargain. Wanted to exchange rubles or Soviet gifts for USA clothes or dollars.

JetCapade staffers also were approached in Mexico, Brazil, Cuba, Poland, and Vietnam. A uniformed Rio policeman offered—and exchanged—money for JetCapade reporters at the airport. And it wasn't a setup.

"Nobody respects the law in Brazil," said Moses Henrique, forty-one, a Rio souvenir shop owner who changes money illegally. He was including himself.

"But I wouldn't [exchange money illegally] with anybody—unless recommended by someone I know," Henrique said.

• Transporting illegal immigrants across borders is big bucks. Mexicans and Central Americans pay hundreds of dollars for smugglers to carry them across canals or hide them in cars to get past immigration officials.

But police in many countries are fighting back against these and other crimes. Three examples:

• In Manila's red-light district, police have arrested more than two hundred managers of nightclubs, massage houses, and "love motels"—many fronts for prostitution. Over twenty have been closed.

Manila Police Chief Alfredo Lim wants to turn the area into a family-style Disneyland where prostitutes could sell ice cream and flowers.

"Let's be practical," said Susan Bidol, twenty-two, a former bar girl dancer and now a nightclub assistant manager. "Girls here didn't finish high school or elementary school. On a good night, a dancer can make $100. But a flower seller only makes $1 a flower. These girls have a family to support, parents to support. College graduates can't even get jobs here."

Responded Lim: "People said we should not deprive these girls of a living. If that's true, then police should no longer run in pickpockets and burglars."

• In China—where crime is up a reported 35 percent since 1987—elder statesman Deng Xiaoping is calling for harsher punishments. Meaning: more executions.

Since August 1983, when Deng launched an anticrime drive, more than ten thousand Chinese have been executed for their crimes. But more, he said, is needed.

"Generally speaking, the problem now is that we are too

soft on criminals," Deng said. "Execution is one of the indispensable means of education."

It is widely believed that families of the condemned in China must even pay 27 cents for the bullet.

• Great Britain and the USA have imposed tough security measures for USA airline flights from 103 airports in the Middle East and Western Europe. They include airport bomb-detection devices; the X-ray or physical inspection of all checked baggage; and denying passengers access to their luggage after the additional security checks.

This in response to the December 1988 bombing of a Pan American World Airways 747 that killed all 259 people over Lockerbie, Scotland, and eleven people on the ground. Terrorism was blamed.

London author Nick Danziger, thirty, flew that same Pan Am flight the day before it was bombed. "I'm overly paranoid," he told us. "You now have to start on the premise that you cannot trust anyone. Your security is never guaranteed."

That seems to be true everywhere. But countries are trying to fight back. To put a dent in a billion-dollar industry threatening every corner and country in the world. To allow people trapped inside their homes to walk freely without fear of the dark. To calm a frightened world.

But they have a long way to go. Maybe further than they think.

Just ask professional thief Ailton Games da Silva. A good criminal, he said, will never be caught. "We're too slippery."

**"Crime of Century" Made Him Famous**

Ronald Arthur Biggs—tanned, handsome, and living the good life—is a celebrity in Brazil.

People wave and nod to him on the street. Ask him for autographs, pictures. Even pay $200 apiece to spend twelve hours with him.

There's more.

He gets fan mail addressed to "The Honorable Ronald Biggs of the Great Train Robbery, Rio de Janeiro, Brazil." Is regularly interviewed for worldwide papers and magazines. Has written his autobiography, *My Own Story*. Has been the subject of two movies. Even sang on a record with the Sex Pistols, a rock band.

"All things considered, I live a very good life here," he said at his Rio home. Nearby: his pool table and backyard swimming pool.

Biggs, fifty-five, is a crook. A train robber. A lawbreaker. A thief. And loving every minute of it.

He took part in Britain's "Great Train Robbery"—as it came to be known—on August 8, 1963. He and fifteen others stopped a train at 3 A.M. in Shires Crossing, England. Got away with $7.3 million. Biggs' cut: $400,000. London papers exclaimed it the "crime of the century."

He was sentenced to thirty years in prison. Escaped after two. Failed attempts to recapture him—in 1974 and 1981—only increased his popularity.

The first: A Scotland Yard official knocked on Bigg's Rio hotel room door. Arrested him. But failed to check on whether Brazil and Great Britain had an extradition treaty. They didn't.

Then Biggs' girlfriend, Raimunda Rothen, announced she was carrying Biggs' child. Under Brazilian law, the parent of a Brazilian child cannot be deported. Biggs lucked out again.

Second attempt: Two men accosted Biggs in a restaurant. Dragged him into a waiting van. Gagged and blindfolded him. Put him on a Learjet and then a yacht bound for Barbados.

Brazilian officials were angered. A Barbados lawyer stepped in. Said Biggs' kidnappers—dispatched by a private London detective—hadn't followed proper extradition procedures. The magistrate released Biggs. He arrived in Rio. Kissed the ground as thousands of Brazilians cheered. Their hero had returned.

"I've been lucky," Biggs told us. "Someone heavenly is watching over me."

While in Rio, Biggs is not allowed to work or go to bars. He must check in with local police twice a week. That hardly cramps his style.

His only foreseeable problem: In 1992, his son, Michael, will no longer be a minor. Biggs could lose an important defense against deportation.

"I don't know what's going to happen after that," Biggs said. "I will play the cards dealt me and make the best of the situation."

But that's not his biggest worry. Foremost on his mind: "Whether the movie [about his escape] will be a success" and whether his new T-shirts will sell.

Their message: I KNOW SOMEONE WHO WENT TO BRAZIL AND MET RONNIE BIGGS—HONEST! Price: $10.

Sometimes, crime pays.

———

### Global Gangsters Gang Up on Law and Order

Chikara Masuda, twenty-four, grimaces in pain as an artist begins tattooing a gun into his arm.

"This is to prove that I have dedicated my life to the Yamaguchi-gumi," Masuda said, gritting his teeth.

It's a process he will endure three times weekly for three months until most of his body is covered with tattoos.

The tattoos are a sign of loyalty and

pride in the Yamaguchi-gumi—Japan's largest Mafia-style gang-ster group.

"My organization is of the highest priority—even though I love Japan, too," Masuda said.

The Japanese Mafia—called *yakuza,* a term derived from the lucky dice combination of eight, nine, and three—is boom-ing. Both in Japan and the USA. They're reportedly involved in sales of stimulants, gambling, prostitution, and nightclub "pro-tection" rackets. Despite police efforts.

Japan's gangs number thirty-one hundred clans. Claim eighty-six thousand—possibly up to a hundred twenty thou-sand—members. Account for one-third of those accused of murder in Japan. Sixty percent of those arrested for blackmail.

They've been around for years. Trace their origins to un-employed seventeenth century samurai.

In Japan—a country known for law and order—the *yakuza* operate openly in small headquarters thinly disguised as con-struction companies. Or not disguised at all. Much to the chagrin of local residents.

But citizens have fought—and are fighting—back in Japan and Italy. Elsewhere, like the Soviet Union, mob influence and violence is spreading—out of control.

• Japan: In March 1988, residents of Ebitsuka, a neighbor-hood in the city of Hamamatsu—130 miles southwest of Tokyo—forced the *yakuza* to leave their area after a three-year battle.

Citizens built a two-level shack across the street from the gangster's five-story green building. Videotaped everyone who came and went: Men in flashy, designer suits, dark glasses, short-cropped hair, and multicolored tattoos.

Shop owners refused to sell goods to the *yakuza.* Residents protested daily. Lodged a lawsuit against them.

But the gangsters fought back. They smashed windows. Stabbed the Ebitsuka's lawyer. Slashed a resident's throat.

The battle gained national media attention. Ebitsuka's eight-man police force got help from three hundred other officers. Gangsters were jailed. Placed under detention.

Eventually, the *yakuza* conceded. Agreed to an out-of-court settlement. Moved out. Residents rejoiced. Claimed victory.

• Italy: In Palermo, Sicily—home of the famed and powerful Italian Mafia—338 organized crime members were convicted in December 1988. Allowing residents to breathe a sigh of relief.

"Once we were of the opinion that the Mafia was like the landscape," said Palermo, Sicily, Mayor Leoluca Orlando.

"Now a growing number are saying it's time to put an end to the Mafia," said Italian State Prosecutor Giuseppe Ayala. Residents have termed the city's new mood *Palermo Primavera*—Palermo spring.

But the battle has taken a toll. Orlando said he lives "a completely peculiar life. I don't drive a car. I always have five bodyguards."

Same thing for Ayala: "I've forgotten what it's like to go for a walk to buy a newspaper," he said.

Both men say the sacrifices have been worth it.

"Palermo can be a model for our country," Orlando said.

But Ayala offered a word of warning: "You can't underestimate the power of the international Mafia."

• Soviet Union: Mobsters are extorting millions from the country's new cooperative restaurant owners and others, according to the globe's newest capitalists.

Demanding "protection money" to allow the co-ops to exist peacefully. Leaving co-op owners helpless—and afraid to speak out.

If Soviet mobsters don't get what they want, the mobsters kill, beat, or threaten owners, families, and relatives, co-op owners said. Even blow up the shops.

"If I had known what this was going to be like before I started, I never would have gotten into it," a co-op owner who requested anonymity said in a published interview. "Now I have to fear for my wife and my child and my business."

Mobsters also are involved in selling Western goods to Soviet citizens at exorbitant prices: cigarettes, $80 a pack; shoes, $400 a pair.

Deal in drugs, gambling, racketeering, prostitution, and pornography. Run burglary rings earning up to $3.2 million a year. Pay hit men up to $160,000 a contract.

Bribe high-ranking government officials $1.6 million to operate freely. All according to the Soviet newspapers *Literaturnaya Gazetta* and *Moskovsky Komsomolets.*

Only 20 percent of convicted felons go to prison, said the Moscow criminal investigation department. Reason: Mobsters are paying off—or collaborating—with police, said Soviet Interior Minister Vadim Bakatin.

"The greatest difference between the Mafia in the United States and the Soviet Union is that in America, they tend to move into peripheral, illegal activities like prostitution, drugs, gambling," said Soviet historian Roy Medvedev in a published interview.

"Here, they are into everything."

Police, beset by low budgets and lack of personnel and equipment, are little threat to the mobsters.

Example: Soviet police drive underpowered Soviet-made cars, are allotted eighty gallons of gas a month. Mobsters drive large imported cars with police-band radios.

Said a Soviet senior criminal investigator, Sergei Kozghanov, in a published interview: "What sort of serious fight can we be leading if the Mafiosi are even better equipped than we are?"

**Illegal Gun Business Keeps Town Alive**

You may not find Danao, Philippines, on many maps. But it has a worldwide reputation. Just ask any gangster. Or gun collector.

This thriving town of sixty thousand north of Cebu in the central Philippines churns out hundreds of cheap guns a year.

Many are imitations of more expensive brands. Like some of the ones marked "Smith and Wesson, Springfield, Mass."

They shoot 5.56-caliber bullets. Just like the U.S. military's M-16.

"It's a Danao product," said gun factory worker Alfredo Bayo, who offered to sell us one for $50. "It's made nowhere else in the world."

Anyone can buy a Danao—as they're called—for as little as $30. There are all makes—or "fake" makes—and models.

But the big orders come from Manila middlemen who buy for Japanese gangsters.

"They like to buy five-shot police .38 revolvers," Bayo said. "A motorboat once picked up five sacks containing a hundred revolvers each. They paid for them first and gave us five months to produce them."

This illicit gun-producing town—80 percent of the residents are involved in the business—is the country's largest.

How do they get away with it?

"It's a cottage industry here," said Danao mayor and old-time warlord Ramon Durano. "If you take it away from the people, then they cannot survive."

Said Felix Capuyan, twenty-six, who boasted he could make a .38-caliber revolver in four days: "There is no other job for me. You don't get anything from fishing or farming."

But the real reason for the town's existence is Durano himself. He rules Danao with an iron fist. Police, army, and government officials stay clear. No one threatens him—not even his sons.

When son Tadeo challenged his father for the mayorship, Tadeo was mysteriously shot. Family members now say Tadeo "is on a long vacation."

"We like [Durano] because we can run to him for our problems," said Francisco Isidro, Jr., twenty-six, who runs gun parts from manufacturer to assembler. "From birth to death, he takes care of you."

And your gun needs.

Said Bayo, still trying to sell us a gun:

"We make them look just like the originals."

***Crime Ignores International Borders***

Crime has taken much of the world hostage.

Changed our lifestyles. Increased our awareness.

Crime, unfortunately, is one of the things we share around the world.

Some countries are successfully fighting back. Others find themselves overwhelmed. It's a multibillion-dollar industry that stretches into every country and corner—and shows no sign of easing up.

Said Nick Danziger, "Your security in this world is no longer guaranteed."

CHAPTER 13

# Faith Flourishes
# Around the World

Religion is an inseparable part of the lives of millions of
people, especially those at Jerusalem's "Wailing Wall," who
pray for God's help, wisdom, and strength.
Photo: Callie Shell, *Nashville Tennessean*

A BD al-Karim al-Qimari started praying in the middle of our interview. He bowed his head, covered his face with his hands. Prayed quietly in Arabic in Old Jerusalem:

"I believe in God. May He be praised. May God be praised."

Other Moslems joined in. The noise around us died down. The bustling marketplace in front of the Damascus Gate in the walled city had turned into a mini-mosque.

All we did was ask: How important is your faith?

Al-Qimari explained: It's not uncommon to break out in prayer. His faith was everything to him. To everybody in Israel and its occupied territories.

"If these walls could speak, you would hear the history of man," said al-Qimari, thirty-six, who sells *zibda,* a cream made from sheep's milk.

"This is the sacred city for all faiths," he said. "In this city, we have something in common."

In all cities. All countries. All continents. Religion plays a key role. For billions, it means hope. Security. Salvation.

Religion is expressed publicly and privately in thousands of ways:

- From preaching and proselytizing
- To fasting and feasting
- From Jerusalem and Johannesburg
- To Rio and Rome

"There is a hunger all over the world for God," evangelist Billy Graham told us in China. "For purpose and meaning in life. Especially among young people."

He should know. He's preached to over a hundred million people since 1940. Still going strong.

The hunger and excitement for faith—expressed different ways—is still strong, too.

Just ask Mary Prisant, thirty-six, of Cincinnati, Ohio.

She traveled to Rome with her Assumption Church Choir to sing before Pope John Paul II.

One of thirteen thousand cheering, clapping, and crying people at his weekly audience.

They came from all over world. All trying to reach out and touch "Papa" as he walked by. He responded by wiping the tears of the elderly, hugging the disabled, and kissing the kids.

Prisant had been looking forward to the experience for two years. She was nearly overcome with emotion when she sang.

"I never dreamed it would be this beautiful," she said immediately after singing. "The memories of him reaching out to people and me touching him. It's a miracle. Every Catholic should experience this. It will bring them closer to God."

In one way or another, people around the world echoed what Father Andrea Martini, seventy-one, of Rome, told us:

"Our faith is personal. That's what makes it special. We each have our own calling."

Take Sister Maria Dolores, seventy-nine, of Salzburg, Austria. A cloistered nun for fifty-five years in the twelve-hundred-year-old Nonnberg Abbey in the Austrian Alps. Famed as the abbey where Maria Von Trapp of *The Sound of Music* spent time.

Sister Dolores rarely gets out. But couldn't be happier. She's short, sweet, sunny, and spunky. Quick as a whip. Light blue eyes. Dark black habit.

"I've been happy from the first day until now," she said in perfect English. "This is a life commitment. It's like a marriage."

And then there's Radha Krishan, fifty-five, a Hindu priest at New Delhi, India's Birla Mandir Temple. Just as excited about his religion.

"We give the statues of the gods and goddesses a bath, pray to them, collect the bath water which is our holy water," Krishan said. "For me, these statues are not just stone, they're alive. I treat them like they're living entities."

His fellow worshippers come to the temple for peace of mind, Krishan said. "They come here when they're troubled. When they have problems. Or to pray to God to say 'Look, I've sinned. Forgive me' or 'I have a problem, please take it away.' They come. They ask for something. When they get it, they come back to give thanks."

Regardless of how—or what—they worship, many people told us attendance at their services is growing. The Yoido Full Gospel Central Church in Seoul, South Korea, was an example:

• In 1958, it had five followers. Today, it's the world's largest Christian church: 530,000-plus members.

• Each Sunday, seven packed services. Each with twenty-five thousand people. Another twenty-five thousand watching by video broadcast. Fifteen sanctuaries. Sixty thousand home fellowship/prayer groups.

But, the pastor, the Reverend Paul Yonggi Cho, warned: "Success is measured in faith, not in volume."

As we traveled around the world, we also were reminded that:

• Religion not only binds but separates.

Wars based on religion: Northern Ireland, where it's Catholics vs. Protestants; India, Sikhs vs. Hindus; and the Middle East, where Muslims, Jews, and Christians fight each other— and often among themselves.

Some governments try to suppress faith, but can't stop it.

Case in point: Poland. Official religion: atheism. People: 95 percent Catholic. Churches dot the countryside. Dominate city neighborhoods.

"The church here remains a factor of stability and reliability," said Father Jerzy Dabrowski in Warsaw.

The church has often pitted itself against the government. Chief church symbols: Polish Pope John Paul II and slain Solidarity priest Jerzy Popieluszko.

The Pope is the second most popular person in Poland behind Soviet leader Mikhail Gorbachev. He leads the way for religious and political reform.

• People are willing to risk their freedom for what they believe.

Another case in point: the Soviet Union. Like Poland, it's officially atheist. But also like Poland, religious faith is strong. Only here the church is primarily an underground institution.

The international human rights group Keston College of England estimates that over a hundred fifty Christians are in labor camps because of their faith. Despite glasnost. Despite perestroika.

"It's very difficult to be a priest in the Soviet Union," said the Reverend Valentin Dronov in Moscow. "The first problem is that of a priest dealing with the souls of believers. Second, the problem dealing with the government."

• The church's role can be as political as it is religious.

Forefront of religious controversy: Archbishop Desmond Tutu of South Africa. Leading the fight against apartheid. Loved by many. Hated by others.

"I'm guided in my actions by what I believe to be right and not by the numbers of people I may happen to speak for," Tutu told us.

South Africa President Pieter W. Botha said of Tutu: "He is not representative of the majority of Christians in South Africa. He represents less than ten percent. The world makes too much of him."

Botha's government has banned some religious meetings.

And the Reverend Allan Boesak, also a Botha adversary, says:

"When you go to such public meetings, you take your life in your hands."

But no matter how tense oppression and opposition might get around the world, faith remains strong:

A recent Gallup/European Value Systems Group survey of people in twenty-four nations found that people in nineteen of them have a stronger than average faith in God. Highest: Malta, 9.58 on a scale of 10. Lowest: Sweden: 3.99. Others: USA: 8.21; Japan: 4.83.

And according to religious author and expert David B. Barrett, there are over 3.5 billion people practicing some form of worship in the world today—more than ever.

Largest group: Christians—1.64 billion. Up from 32.4 to 33 percent of the world's population in 1986, the latest year figures are available.

Reason: Rapid growth of the Chinese Christian church. Christians in China account for more than fifty-two million of the world's Christians.

Here are the major forms of worship around the world. All except Hinduism showed membership increases in 1986–87:

• Christianity: over 1.64 billion followers; founded by Jesus Christ in 33 A.D.

• Islam: 854 million followers; founded by Muhammad in the 600s A.D.

• Hinduism: 658 million followers; founded by the Aryans and Dravidians in 1500 B.C.

• Buddhism: 312 million followers; founded by Siddhartha Gautama (Buddha) in the late 500s B.C.

• Judaism: 18.2 million followers; founded by Abraham before 2000 B.C.

Three people, from three very different parts of the world, summed it up for JetCapade:

• "You can feel here that young people faced with a difficult situation find a point of hope [in religion]. Hope for Poland. Hope for a better future"—Andrzej Ignarski, twenty-three, of Warsaw, at church.

• "Instead of going after drugs, instead of going into discos, people are turning to religious values"—Ahmed Emad Eldin Aboul-Nasr, sixty-six, University of Cairo professor.

• "Nothing that's ever been devised can stop the church"—Billy Graham.

### *"This Is the Closest Anyone Can Get to God"*

José Torres, twenty-eight, was walking to the shrine of Our Lady of Guadalupe in Mexico City—on his knees.

So were Hermelinda Ortiz Sánchez and thousands of other pilgrims.

Most come at least once a year to plead, praise, or thank the Lady—on their knees—as an act of devotion.

"When my son was born, there were problems . . . and my wife, she was dying. I came here and asked the Virgin to save at least one of them," said Torres, of Mexico City. "She did, so now I will pay her back by doing this the rest of my life."

His wife died. His son, José, Jr., now four, also was walking the hundred yards from the gate to the altar.

"We don't want the Virgin to think we have forgotten what she did for us," Torres added.

According to legend, the Virgin appeared to an Indian named Juan Diego in December 1531. She asked him to build a church to honor her.

When no one believed Diego, the Virgin reappeared. As proof, she gave him some roses—which couldn't be grown among the rocks—and put her image on his cloak. The cloak is on display in the shrine in northern Mexico City.

That was the first miracle.

Since then, "there have been millions of miracles performed by the Virgin, and we want to pay our respects," Sánchez said.

"This is the closest anyone can get to God."

### Just the Way the Gods Like It

They come bearing gifts: fruit, vegetables, candy, even full-course meals.

Some eat in the gods' presence. Others leave food for the temple's workers.

"It's our way of worshiping," explained Buddhist Johnnie Chew at the Tian Hock Keng Temple (or Temple of Heavenly Happiness) in Singapore.

Here, Chew and hundreds of other Buddhists silently offer their required twice-monthly prayers, gifts, and offerings to the Taoist and Buddhist gods of wealth, riches, and wisdom.

The faithful light incense and long red or white candles to symbolize hope that the year is full of light, Chew told us. They do so at five different altars now covered with bowls of apples and oranges.

The temple, Singapore's oldest, was built in 1841. It's where newly arrived immigrants came to offer prayers of thanksgiving for a safe trip.

Chew was one of them. He came to Singapore from Malaysia in 1942 for an education and stayed. Visited the temple upon his arrival to give thanks.

He now works as a tour guide throughout the city but, like many Buddhists, volunteers at the temple. It's his service to the gods.

The temple was brought over in pieces from Amoy, China.

It looks like it's straight out of the award-winning movie *The Last Emperor.* Sloping sharp roofs with intricate pagoda-style architecture; red balloonlike lights hanging from colorful ceilings; altars made of wood and stone and flanked by large vases; stone pillars carved in the shape of dragons; a stone-tiled floor with flowered designs.

It's just the way the gods like it, Chew told us. And what the gods want, they get, he said.

### "We Are All Brothers"

This is the "other" Holy Land. The one in Egypt.

Home to the Reverend Gabriel George Bestavros and the Rabbi Abraham Mosha (Cohen).

Both in love with God and their churches or temples.

Both spending their lives caring for and sharing the history of their churches with whomever will listen.

Both in the minority in Egypt, a predominantly Muslim country.

"I was born in Old Cairo and have been in this church for twenty-two years," said Bestavros, fifty-one, pastor of St. Sergius Church. "In a cave beneath this church, Joseph, Mary, and the infant Jesus lived for three months when they fled from Herod into Egypt."

"This is the Holy Land of Egypt," Bestavros told us. He is a Coptic priest. The Copts are one of the oldest Christian sects in the world.

Nearby is Egypt's oldest synagogue, Ben Ezra, surrounded by twenty-nine mosques and twenty churches. Home to an ancient Torah written on deer skin about 475 B.C.

"I have been here at the temple for forty years," said Mosha, who goes by Rabbi Cohen (meaning servant of the temple). "On this site stood the temple of the prophet Jeremiah. Underneath, you can see the spring where Pharaoh's daughter found Moses in the bushes."

Bestavros said he has been to Long Island and Brooklyn, New York, and California. Rabbi Cohen has never been out of Egypt.

But both agree on one thing: They will never leave their places of worship or their land.

There's also one other thing they agree on, told best in the words of guide Mohamed Khalek, a Muslim: "Here, there is no difference between Christian and Moslems. We are all brothers in Christ."

"For this is the Holy Land of Egypt," Bestavros said.

—

### Dogged Dogma Defies Defeat

—

Fidel Castro was blunt when he told us: You cannot be both a Christian and a socialist. Or at least not yet.

But Monsignor Carlos Manuel de Cespedes and other Cuban priests are finding ways to work around the religion required by Cuba's government, atheism.

"Catholic parents who want a Catholic education for their children bring them to the church on Saturday and Sunday. We do whatever we can do in just a few hours," de Cespedes, fifty-one, said.

De Cespedes is even optimistic. He says the Catholic church is growing. He cites as proof:

• One third of Cuba's newborn are now being baptized.

• More than half of all funerals are Catholic.

• One percent—a hundred thousand of Cuba's ten million people attend Mass regularly, despite the obstacles.

Small signs—but encouraging ones for de Cespedes.

"The main question for Cuban Catholics: exploring the possibility of being Christian without having problems with the Christian identity as the government defines it," he told us. "And at the same time to work and live in Cuba without being identified with the official ideology of the government."

But despite de Cespedes' upbeat determination, thirty years of communism have taken a toll. He admits that:

• Before communism, there were 362 Catholic and Protestant churches. Today, almost all stand as nearly empty reminders of times past. Castro claims he hasn't closed any.

• Before communism, 15 percent of Catholics attended church regularly. Today, only 1 percent.

• Before communism, there were 333 parochial schools. Today, there are none.

Said de Cespedes:

"After almost thirty years of revolution, I believe it is time . . . to grant liberty of expression."

**Millions Practice What He Preaches**

Perched on a cyprus stump alongside Florida's Hillsborough River near West Palm Beach, Billy Graham fixed his piercing blue eyes on his audience and preached.

Sometimes the audience grunted back, Graham remembers. Most of the time, they sat motionless.

His flock: alligators.

From those humble beginnings in 1940, he's gone on to preach in sixty-four foreign countries—including the Soviet Union—to over a hundred million people. Some say he's been seen and heard by more people than anyone in history.

We caught up with Graham in China, where he was visiting his wife Ruth's hometown, Qingjiang. He also was giving lectures and preaching at small church gatherings.

Today he's seventy. A thirty-year veteran of the international preaching circuit.

"When I go down steps, I hold on to the rail," he said. "I'd like to slow down, do reading and writing. But I don't think that will happen. I feel God calling me to keep on preaching."

A possible future Billy Graham crusade: China.

He said Christianity thrives in China despite oppressions as recent as a year ago. Maintains China's Cultural Revolution may even have helped Christianity:

"People went to their homes and they established house churches." There are an estimated fifty-two million Chinese Christians.

Graham cringes at the world's "suffering and immorality, the fraud and all the things going on."

But he has reason to hope: The nuclear arms control pact signed by President Ronald Reagan and Soviet General Secretary Mikhail Gorbachev is a small step but an important one.

Another reason: a growing revival in parts of the world. Such as in Eastern and Western Europe—site of recent crusades.

"Some nights, even before I started the invitation to accept Christ, they started running forward. And they came by the thousands.

"Young people are searching for a way out. From their point of view, we're leaving them a terrible world. With atomic bombs. Big deficits. A lot of crime. And a lot of drugs. And many of these young people see no way out."

As we concluded our time with Graham, we asked him how he would like to be remembered.

"As a preacher of the Gospel. That I had opportunities to do other things. But that I never deviated."

———

### Art Gives Him a Chance to Spread the Word

Father Andrea Martini's church, St. Bartholemew, is famous not only in Rome, but in all of Europe.

It was built in the first century, making it one of the oldest Catholic churches.

Tourists regularly stop by to admire its ancient architecture.

But the real prize is in the basement. Something an all too humble Martini doesn't show tourists.

It's his sculpture garden, housing Martini's world-renowned works of art. Sculptures of athletes, Biblical scenes and figures, and people who have touched his life.

Sculptures—or pictures of them—that are on display in churches and museums worldwide, have been part of the personal collections of the last six popes, and are the subjects of postage stamps, postcards, and countless books.

All hailed as some of finest in the world.

"I have a double calling," said Martini. "I preach and create the words of God through my art. I have a chance to approach the world in ways other priests don't."

Martini spends his days celebrating Mass, counseling his congregation, and creating his masterpieces. He told us he often uses his sculptures to bring across certain points in counseling sessions.

Such as one of an Olympic bicyclist whose face shows the anguish and pain of his effort. "This tells us we must always persevere."

Or the sculpture of Jesus on the cross. He uses that one to share his faith.

"Muslims, Baptists, Japanese Shinto. They all come here," he said. "Art gives me a chance to spread the Christian word."

Martini's a short, chubby, balding, gentle Franciscan priest.

He speaks slowly—very slowly. Always holds your hand as he talks—except when he needs his to make a point. Always smiling. Always making you feel at ease. Showing you he cares.

But try to compliment his work, and he looks down. He nods his head to acknowledge your praise—but appears almost embarrassed.

"I am just His servant," Martini said. "He gave me the gift. So, I compliment Him."

———

**Religion Around the World**

———

Religion is clearly a common denominator around the world. It's expressed in many different ways but, in most cases, to the same God. No matter what the form, it's an expression of faith. Here are some inescapable impressions of people and religion around the world:

• Saudi Arabia: Moslems praying five times a day for ten minutes. Services on Friday. Times listed in the newspaper. Businesses close. Work stops.

- Pago Pago, American Samoa: Packed Assembly of God services in hundred-plus degree tropical temperatures. No air conditioning. No complaining.
- India: Vagrant cows causing traffic jams. Hindus won't push the cows out of the way, because they are honored and considered godlike.
- Philippines: Small shrines to the Virgin Mary along roadsides, in shops, airports. With flowers, Bible, holy water. Catholics kneel and pray.
- Costa Rica: Jimmy Swaggart's evangelistic crusades are feeding poor, housing homeless, converting thousands. Shacks are equipped with TV antennas, satellite dishes to watch the show.
- Brazil: A ninety-nine-foot-tall statue of Jesus stands on Corcovado Mountain. Looks ominously down on city, arms open. Embracing city, embracing people.
- Taiwan: President Lee Teng-hui, sixty-five. Strong, outspoken Christian. In a predominantly Buddhist country. Wants to be a missionary.
- Egypt: Sphered mosques, two or three to a city block. Some adorned with gold. All adored with reverence.
- Japan: Giant Buddhas for worship in the city, tiny Buddhas for sale in shops. Adults worship, kids buy.
- Austria: Benedictine monks and cloistered nuns singing in abbeys on Sunday morning. Hills alive with the sound of music.

Religion clearly is a guiding light that continues to shine. For billions, it's a hospice of hope defended with devotion.

# CHAPTER 14

# Making the World a Better Place

Much of the world survives on good will. Thanks to people
like Mother Teresa—the "Saint of Calcutta"—who cares for
thousands of people, one by one.

Photo: Mary Ellen Mark Library

T HE sun has just risen in Calcutta. But you couldn't tell from inside the Home for the Destitute and Dying: The sun doesn't shine here.

Inside a dark room—full of the strong stench of disinfectant—Agnes Gonxha Bojaxhiu, seventy-nine, goes about her daily work.

Inside the home, they call her the Saint of Calcutta.

To the world, she is Mother Teresa.

She walks up to each of the blue-painted steel cots lining the bare walls. Serves their sickly occupants breakfast. An omelet. A glass of milk.

But many are too sick to eat. They are lepers. Abandoned adults. Homeless children. All too sick even to walk the concrete floor. Living out their last days.

Still, the small, stooped peasant woman, dressed in white sari and sandals, cheerfully talks with them—though few are able to answer. Touches them—though few respond.

She straightens their beds. Washes them. Prays for them. Loves them.

They are here—not on the streets—because Bojaxhiu cares. She and her staff give them free medical care, food, and if possible an education. Ask nothing in return.

The sick, orphaned, abandoned, desperate, and dying— over fifty thousand since 1952—have been Bojaxhiu's family for thirty-seven years. Many die, but many walk out healthy. To live on their own.

She is a mother to them—"the poorest of the poor"—and thousands more like them around the world. A light in the midst of darkness. A candle of hope.

There are more like her. Serving in villages. In hospitals. In ghettos. In every corner of the world. Helping the poor. The sick. The forgotten. The needy. Giving their time, money, and lives unselfishly for others.

And their numbers seem to be on the rise:

• Mother Teresa's Missionaries of Charity order of nuns now has eleven hundred sisters and forty thousand volunteer coworkers in three hundred fifty missions in eighty countries. She started in 1950 with a total staff of twelve in Calcutta.

• The Peace Corps is well on its way to doubling its membership to ten thousand by 1992 from its current fifty-two hundred according to director Loret Miller Ruppe, sixty-three.

• And Action, a U.S. federal volunteer agency, is "seeing an increase in volunteerism in all our populations. . . . Numbers are growing," said director Donna Alvarado, thirty-nine.

Reason: People want more out of life—an inner peace— that comes with giving, Mother Teresa has said.

And our increased efforts seem to be making some dent in at least one area: world hunger.

Number of people dying from world hunger in 1979: forty-one thousand. Number in 1989: thirty-five thousand.

"It's still far too many people, but it shows we are closing in on the issue," said actress Valerie Harper, forty-seven, spokesperson for the End Hunger Network, an international group. "There is a whole shift in policy that needs to occur and that's starting."

Harper is one of many celebrities banning together for charity work around the world.

Many of those giving to others, like Mother Teresa, get lots of publicity. Others, like Peace Corps volunteer Andrew Karas, twenty-seven, in Voi, Kenya, are known only to the people they serve.

"The responsibility has been pretty awesome at times," Karas said. "You really feel you have a lot of people counting on you. I measure my effectiveness by how well they do. If they succeed, I feel I've succeeded."

They have.

Karas taught the women of Voi to build fuel-efficient stoves. Raise chickens. Harvest honey. Braid baskets. Then sell what they've made for profit. Much-needed money for the village.

The Kenyans nicknamed Karas "Mwadime"—Swahili for "person who brings light."

"Thank God for bringing Andrew to Kenya," said Mercy Nyange, thirty, chairwoman of the Kishamba Women's Group near Voi. "He gave us the heart . . . the courage to undertake projects we wouldn't have undertaken."

But Karas' service—like that of other volunteers around the world—does more than just help the people he works with:

• It builds bridges between people and countries.

What better ambassador could a country have and what better understanding could he take back than this?" said Kenya Peace Corps director James Beck, fifty-four.

Case in point: A 1989 earthquake in Soviet Armenia brought an outpouring of international assistance—unmatched since the post–World War II period—from many noncommunist countries around the world.

West Germany sent four cargo planes of food, medical supplies, and rescue experts. The USA sent three. Great Britain, two.

France sent two hundred doctors and rescue workers.

India, a forty-two-member medical team. Cuba, blood. Pope John Paul II, a $100,000 contribution. And South Korea offered to send "all possible human and material assistance."

The effort crossed cultural and political boundaries: The help came even though neither the Vatican nor South Korea has diplomatic ties with the Soviet Union.

And there was much more from individuals, groups like the Red Cross, and other countries.

These and other efforts, charity groups say, demonstrate that giving is not—and never should be—predicated on race, politics, or religious beliefs.

"White, brown, green, or yellow, people are all children of God," Mother Teresa said in an interview in early 1989.

Take Christopher George, director of the West Bank/Gaza Strip office of Save the Children.

Who is right or wrong in the struggle over Palestine is less important to George than who is getting hurt. George and his staff are trying to save the children injured in the battle by setting up clinics, working on water and sewer projects, and conducting mother-child workshops.

It's an uphill battle because of the war. One that stretches him and his staff daily.

"I have seen children kicked and clubbed . . . imprisoned without being charged, deprived of education," George said. "In light of what we've seen, we feel we have to speak out."

Even one of the federation's workers was pulled from his car and beaten. Still, Save the Children continues its work.

• It picks up where governments left off. Fills in where they can't—or won't—be.

Example: USA For Africa, Band Aid, and Live Aid—fund-raising rock concerts and celebrity-backed donation campaigns for thousands dying of starvation in Africa in the 1980s.

The Ethiopian government couldn't—or wouldn't—do enough. So British rocker Bob Geldof decided he had to.

How he got the idea was simple enough: He was watching the news. A BBC documentary about the famine.

Suddenly it hit him.

"I was utterly speechless," Geldof, thirty-three, said.

He began by writing a song about the famine. Solicited help from fellow musicians and producers. He then took his song to the airwaves.

People around the world contributed over $100 million. Much of it in pennies and nickels. Nearly all of it was delivered in food to Africa. His work spawned similar efforts around the world. Saved thousands of lives. Raised the world's consciousness.

But Geldof and others say small, local, often unnoticed efforts are just as important as the big publicity-getting campaigns.

Their advice: If you see a need, jump in.

That's exactly what Al Sánchez, fifty-nine, did when he moved from Maryland to Antigua, Guatemala, in July 1986. His goal: to start an orphanage for some of Guatemala's 250,000 abandoned or orphaned children.

Previous trips to Guatemala had shown there was a need. A desperate need. Children were being abandoned by their prostitute mothers. Beaten by their drunken fathers. Left outdoors to fend for themselves.

Sánchez packed up his belongings. Gathered private and church donations. Left to help meet the need.

Today, his Prince of Peace Home for Girls houses eighteen girls, ages three to eighteen. Provides them with education, skills, love. For free.

"We are not just taking care of them but strengthening them educationally and spiritually. Making them productive members of society so they can make a difference," said housemother Cindy Miller, fifty-seven, also from Maryland. Up to five more orphanages are planned.

But life is difficult for Sánchez and his assistants in politically unstable Guatemala. They are not paid. Work under third-world conditions. Have no luxuries.

"The only thing that keeps us down here is the need and knowing that God wants us here," he said.

Their inspiration: "Whatsoever you do for the least of these, that you do unto Me."

### *"Give a Little Back"*

Rebo, Man of a Million Tricks, is famous all over South Africa's circus tents.

An illusionist with the Boswell Wilkie Circus. One of the world's best. Draws thousands of fans. Draws thousands of smiles.

"I do it for the cheering," said Rebo, whose real name is Johannes Philippus Oberholzer, sixty-seven, of Kibler Park, South Africa. "There's nothing like hearing the applause, the thunder as you walk out of the ring."

But beyond the big top, the lights, the cheering is another side of Rebo. The one that performs to audiences that sometimes can't clap. Or see. Or hear. Or speak.

They are confined to retirement homes. Hospitals. Orphanages.

And these performances are free.

"I owe humanity. I owe society a lot for keeping me in illusions," Rebo said.

Rebo's reward: Faces that light up. Smiles that burst forth. The satisfaction of helping others. That, he says, is worth more than money—or applause.

"Give a little back, I always believe." That he does.

### *"There Is a Lot of Devastation All Over"*

Ugandan pilot Gad Gasaatura used to be a symbol of terror. People ran whenever he landed his small plane. With good reason. He flew former Ugandan dictator Idi Amin.

Today, it's a different story. Gasaatura—after fleeing his native Uganda for his life in 1977—has returned as a relief pilot. Flying doctors, rescue workers, and supplies into Uganda's remote areas.

He's one of 113 pilots for Mission Aviation Fellowship, an international airborne group providing aerial and communication help to missionaries and relief workers in twenty-six countries.

Gasaatura—who raises his own support, since he isn't paid a salary—flies for World Vision, USAID, Oxfam, African Inland Mission, and the Lutheran World Federation.

"Now I am meeting the needs of people and not threatening them. It's a world of difference," he said.

It's a world of work, too.

"We've had three wars in less than a decade. So there is a lot of devastation all over," Gasaatura said. "Our main thrust right now is helping with relief and development work."

Gasaatura and Mission Aviation Fellowship are one of many pilot groups flying the world.

Australia's Flying Doctors—famous after a TV show was named after them—provide emergency treatment anywhere in Australia, at any time, at no cost. Mostly to aborigines in the country's rugged and remote outback.

And because of the TV show, the real Flying Doctors are enjoying a new popularity—and using it to their advantage.

"We've had ladies here in tears" after they've seen the show, said Diane Newall, director of tourism for the team in Alice Springs, Australia. Tourism? Yes, you read right.

The TV show has attracted such attention that the Flying Doctors Gift Shop now does $185,000 worth of business a year.

And all the money goes into buying planes.

### He Follows in the Footsteps of Dr. Livingstone

Dr. Livingstone, I presume?

That fabled question—made famous in the 1939 movie *Stanley and Livingstone*—lives on in the minds of Spencer Tracy fans.

The subject: Dr. David Livingstone. Scottish missionary doctor. One of the best known early white explorers of Africa. Discoverer of Africa's majestic Victoria Falls. Founder of a Botswanan hospital.

Today that small hospital has grown to 267 beds and provides some of Africa's finest medical care. Thanks to another missionary, Dr. Alfred Merriweather.

But at sixty-nine, Merriweather ends a hundred-fifty-year tradition, begun by Livingstone, of Scottish missionaries in Botswana. "I'm the end of the line," he said.

His accomplishments have been written into history books:

• Immunizing 85 percent of Botswana's children under age six for polio, measles, and tetanus

• Making prenatal care common throughout the country

• Upgrading medical care to include a hundred fifty native-born doctors for the country's one million people

• Acting as personal physician to Botswana's first independent president, Sir Seretse Khama

• Working as speaker of Botswana's National Assembly for five years

Merriweather came to Molepolole in 1944 after serving two and a half years in the Indian army. "They let me go early on the condition I come here directly because of the grave shortage of doctors in Botswana."

He brought little besides his army uniforms, his medical bag, and two Bibles.

Today, he leaves a legacy.

Still, he claimed, Livingstone accomplished more and will always be remembered fondly—especially by Merriweather.

Case in point: Merriweather preaches at Molepolole's

United Congregational Church on Sunday. "And when I mention Livingstone, everyone's eyes light up," Merriweather said.

Including his own. "He was my boyhood hero."

———

***"The Government Needs Our Contribution"***

———

Dr. Mustafa Mahmoud is part Jerry Falwell, TV evangelist; part Carl Sagan, popular author and astronomer; and part Marcus Welby, the wise and amicable TV doctor of days past.

He is Islamic Egypt's TV evangelist, dispensing his brand of fundamentalism on a weekly talk show.

And Mahmoud, sixty-six, has put some substance behind his rhetoric.

He has founded a health center, mosque, and astrological observatory complex in Giza that's attracted considerable attention and support.

The center—supported by private contributions—rivals many government-operated facilities: six kidney dialysis machines, CAT scanners, stress-test devices, and specialized clinics for physical therapy and dentistry.

Average fee for visits: 50 cents. It draws twenty thousand patients a year.

"The government needs our contribution so it can cope with the overpopulation," Mahmoud said. "There are not enough schools, universities, hospitals. We fill the gap."

More is planned: a thirty-bed clinic and a sixty-bed hospital, offering more services and jobs.

As Mahmoud winds his way through the covered paths connecting the clinics, public affection is clear. People and patients rush to shake his hand or touch his arm.

He invites all of them to his lectures on science and religion. To gaze at the heavens from one of three telescopes. Or study volcanic rock and crystal at its geological collection.

"The young are frustrated," he said. "There are not enough chances for them. Chances mean investment. That is what we are doing." In his own way.

**"I'm Angry Every Bloody Day"**

One boy lost a foot. Another, a leg. And another may lose both his hip and leg.

And still others are ill with tuberculosis, worms, and other infections.

"This has become my life," said Peace Corp volunteer Alexander Korff, fifty-five. A life too trying for many people.

Nearly all the boys are outpatients of the malnutrition ward at Western Visayas Hospital in Iloilo, Philippines, the public hospital where Korff works.

Korff is a "facilitator"—helping patients communicate with doctors, deal with government red tape, apply for public assistance, get prescriptions filled.

He opens his house to the hospital's outpatients—until they're strong enough to go home.

It began in 1987 when he took in two boys. One was dying of irreversible malnutrition; the other of cancer.

In April 1988, Korff was named John F. Kennedy Volunteer of the Year for Asia and North Africa—one of three Peace Corp regions. An award he said he didn't need.

"Peace Corps is giving me the opportunity to do exactly what I want to do. And then they give me an award. It's crazy," he said.

Korff, a former Roman Catholic priest, joined the Peace Corps in 1985, teaching Asian refugees English.

"What I'm doing here is priestly work. It does not have to be done in the name of God or Christ to have value," he said.

"It's a matter of social responsibility," Korff said. "We're products of the first world, while two-thirds of the global village is second- and third-world. We're a minority now. Shouldn't we find out what the rest of the world is like?"

But life can be hard and trying for Korff.

"I'm angry every bloody day. I wake up every morning and I'm screaming. Take Robert. He's third-degree malnourished and he's like any other spoiled brat. He won't eat vegetables. They're remarkable and lazy and drive you crazy—because they're kids," Korff said.

Robert is seven, but looks three. Malnutrition has stunted his growth, caused mild brain damage. "He'll never be a doctor of philosophy, but he'll get better," Korff said, with an air of fatherly love.

Korff knows he can't make the boys dependent on him and teaches them how to survive. He does pay school tuition for one boy, who otherwise wouldn't be able to attend:

"I want him to have an opportunity. The tuition is $50 a year. Am I breaking my bank? You can't do everything, so you make judgments. And it makes a difference to Robert and Romeo and Leo."

Korff's experience is leaving him with a lifetime of memories. He told us of one:

"Here, kneeling in the mud, was this ten-year-old fixing his little brother's grave. I'd never seen such concentration. He was up to his ass in mud but all he was concerned about was that this grave was perfect. That the mound was round. It was simply glorious.

"If I were to take the finest moments of my life and put them in a package, I couldn't match that. There are a lot of those times. That's what keeps me here.

"I feel like Gauguin when he went to Tahiti: I've arrived where I belong."

———

### Giving Is Part of Living

———

These anecdotes represent only a handful of the millions of people striving to make the world a better place.

But they each show that the spirit of sharing and caring is alive. That giving is a part of living around the world.

From the individual who collects food to help the homeless to the group organizing large international relief efforts.

We give more than just our time or money; we give ourselves. For the sake of others, who can't survive without us. Because governments can't always fill the need.

But those who give also receive. They get the feeling of satisfaction and peace, knowing that with their lives they are improving the lives of others.

Much of the world survives on goodwill.

# CHAPTER 15

# The Global Village:
# A Conclusion

Global communication has linked the world by satellite,
telephone, TV, and radio. Even this African village in Niger
can plug into the world's news and entertainment with the flip
of a switch on a solar-powered TV.

Photo: © John Chiasson, Gamma Liaison

W E were in a hotel room in Nice, France, and switched on the television. *The Godfather* was on. The same made-in-Hollywood gangster movie we had seen years earlier in the States. With the same English-speaking actors.

But this time, the show also was an example of how interdependent, intertwined, and intercultural the world has become.

Here was a film about Italian-American crime families:

• Shown on the French Riviera, not too far from the Italian border

• Dubbed in German and with French subtitles

• Broadcast from studios in The Netherlands over a cable channel owned by an Australian media mogul who's now a U.S. citizen—Rupert Murdoch

Our world has indeed become smaller.

A global village.

Today, people in hamlets and hotels, countries and continents around the world are connected by:

- 52 communication satellites
- 600 million televisions
- 1 billion radios
- 425 billion telephones

A quarter of a century ago—when there were no communication satellites, no 162 million televisions, no 451 million radios, and no 94 million telephones, media scholar Marshall McLuhan saw the global village coming.

McLuhan argued that instantaneous transmission and reception of information was shrinking the world. "As electrically contracted," he wrote in his 1964 book, *Understanding Media,* "the globe is no more than a village."

He was right. Communications technology, plus high-speed, transworld transportation, international name brands, and small computers, have made the global village a reality. It no longer is a futuristic fantasy.

Ted Turner's Cable News Network is a good example. It calls itself "the world's most important network." A claim that's no doubt debatable. But this is not debatable: What CNN is trying to achieve would not be feasible if not for the age of the global village.

International travelers are well aware that CNN is becoming a worldwide network. It's sort of the globe's town crier.

It's in sixty-seven countries with a potential audience of a hundred million. Next country CNN's expected to sign: The U.S.S.R.

U.S. viewers of CNN can now watch a program called *CNN World Report.* It's the closest thing to a global newscast on TV today. Consists of features and news stories prepared in more than a hundred countries by local journalists.

"Ted Turner had the idea to allow any country to send any news story it wanted, and it would appear unedited as sent. We are doing just that, and it can last from one hour to two and a half hours, and we now have a hundred and five countries contributing," CNN Public Relations Director Jack Womack told us.

Bobbie Battista, one of CNN's anchors, has become a celebrity in Poland. State government drivers assigned to Western visitors often ask if they know her. Some Poles watch CNN just to see her.

MTV—Music Television—also crosses geographic and cultural borders. MTV, which continuously broadcasts music videos, "is one of the most important factors of the global village because it reaches young people over the world in the language of rock 'n' roll," said Robert Poole, president of the Reason Foundation, a public policy think tank in Santa Monica, California.

"You don't have to understand another language in order for kids and teen-agers to feel comfortable with one another across all kinds of borders," Poole said.

There are many more examples:

• *USA Today*'s international edition would not be possible if not for satellite technology. Two satellites are used to beam the newspaper to printing plants in Hong Kong and Singapore, and two other satellites are used to get the paper to a plant near Lucerne, Switzerland.

The international edition is available in more than eighty countries in Western Europe, the Middle East, North Africa, and Asia. Circulation is about fifty thousand a day, with most of the readers being former residents of the USA.

• *Dallas* is considered one of the most-watched—if not the most-watched—TV show on Earth.

• McDonald's can be found in Rome, London, Munich, Mexico City, and Paris. And many other cities outside the USA.

• USA country music is heard around the world.

• Few areas of the world are out of reach of telephone or telex.

• Most areas of the world can be reached in a matter of hours because of jet travel.

• Michael Jackson is a household name from Berlin to Beijing.

What does it all mean?

• "Barriers between countries are coming down," according to Walter R. Roberts, former associate director of the U.S.

Information Agency and now diplomat-in-residence at George Washington University in Washington, D.C.

• "It's not that we are becoming homogenized. We are becoming more tolerant of different ways of life and other cultures—and that's a good thing," Poole said.

Poole even argues that today's high-tech communication can be credited with major political developments—such as glasnost.

"I don't think glasnost results from the goodness of Gorbachev's heart. Glasnost is the product of modern technology, and modern communications in particular," he said.

"When he came to office, Gorbachev faced a clear choice: Either allow personal computers to come into widespread use in the Soviet Union or face oblivion and relegate the Soviet Union to the status of a third-world country," Poole continued.

"Gorbachev chose personal computers. But the implication of all that is that you have to give up central political control over information, and that's why we have glasnost today."

And the Soviet Union isn't the only place affected by the global village, Poole says.

"You are seeing the political effects of low-cost mass communications in the overthrow of [Philippine President Ferdinand] Marcos and [Haitian President Jean-Claude Duvalier] Baby Doc," he said.

"Regimes of crooks and thugs can't really survive the glare of worldwide publicity, and we're going to see more overthrows of dictatorships in the years to come. Dictators can no longer hide what they are doing—either from the rest of the world or their own people."

Les Young, vice president of San Diego–based World Research, Inc., a nonprofit organization dealing with social and educational issues, agrees: "The flow of information is growing to such a degree that it's no longer possible for totalitarian regimes to keep their people from knowing what's going on outside their country."

Jim Carey, chairman of the Department of Communications of the University of Illinois, warns, however, that the cultural blending implied by the term "global village" must not be taken too far.

"Everybody finds something in *Dallas,* but that doesn't make them Texans," Carey said. "You can't assume that wearing certain kinds of clothing and listening to certain kinds of music goes very deep into every person.

"The confrontation with all sorts of products that are made elsewhere—particularly cultural products—also serves to remind people who they are, where they come from, and how different they are from other people.

"The world may be becoming a global village," Carey said, "but it's one in which there are a lot of resentful communities that engage in systematic conflict against this spread."

Example: The initial reaction in 1986 to McDonald's opening in Rome. Fashion designer Valentino complained that McDonald's, which was located at the back of his headquarters, created a "significant and constant noise and an unbearable smell of fried food fouling the air."

He asked Italian magistrates to close it on grounds that it was a nuisance. He got lots of public support. Other critics in Rome labeled McDonald's a "degradation of Rome" and the "Americanization" of Italian culture.

Yet when JetCapade visited two years later, McDonald's was still there. And busy.

Another example: Composer Manos Hadzidakis, sixty-two, in Athens, Greece. He told us that what's really happening in the world today is that countries are losing their identity.

"Greece is not becoming more like the USA or Europe," he said. "Europe is ceasing to be Europe and becoming a team of countries, tending to lose their individuality. In Greece. In France. In Germany. The spirit of decadence is the same in every country. This is the real unity of Europe—the decadence, the loss of meaning."

If what Carey says is true, at most it mitigates the impact of the global village. It certainly doesn't erase it.

Economic interdependence is proof enough.

"The standard cartoon in South Korea is of a U.S. congressman in a French tie, Italian shoes, with a Korean radio and a

Japanese car, speaking out against imports," Horace G. Underwood, seventy, told JetCapade reporters in Seoul. Underwood is assistant to the president of South Korea's Yonsei University.

It's barely a joke. It's not at all unusual in the USA to:

• Drive a car that has a U.S. brand, but was designed in Germany and has an engine from Brazil

• Wear a shirt made in Malaysia, Thailand, or the Dominican Republic and shoes made in Spain or Italy

• Watch the news from around the world on a TV set made in Japan or Korea

The list goes on.

The fact that we are becoming more alike in a number of ways is indisputable. The fact that we might be slightly less mysterious to each other—and slightly less threatening—is promising.

Fewer and fewer countries are isolated from the world. More and more people have a feeling and an appreciation for other cultures.

Yet the world's rich diversity is still there. Should be there. Hopefully, will always be there.

Perhaps Swedish novelist and environmentalist Sara Lidman, sixty-four, put it best when she told us:

"I drink tea from China and the cotton I wear is not from Sweden. Whatever I touch has memories in it of other soils and other people."

It is, indeed, nearly one world.

# Acknowledgments

T HE list of people to be thanked for making this book possible starts with Phil Pruitt, Gannett book editor, and my co-authors, Jack Kelley and Juan J. Walte.

Pruitt generated many of the chapter ideas, fine-tuned and rewrote copy, and in general kept the book on track—in terms of production and quality. He also was the liaison with Doubleday Publishing Company. His invaluable experience as a newspaper editor gave this book the professional direction necessary.

Kelley traveled with me on every mile of the JetCapade journey, and Walte was the senior reporter on one of the JetCapade advance reporting teams. Both worked endless hours on the road and then worked more endless hours helping me write this book. Many thanks to these two top-notch *USA Today* reporters.

The book staff also included researcher/writer Laura E. Chatfield, who contributed many valuable ideas and nitpicked early versions of the manuscript.

Joining the staff for a time were Lynne Perri, a *USA Today* deputy managing editor, who offered editing suggestions on many of the chapters, and Barbara Ries, *USA Today* photographer, who assisted in selecting photographs for the book. Also special thanks to J. Ford Huffman, Gannett News Service Features Editor, and his graphic arts staff, especially Ann LaRose, Carolynne Miller, and John Monahan. I also want to thank Robin Cohen for answering our many questions about the computer system.

The *USA Today* library staff, under manager Dorothy Bland, checked an endless array of facts. Some of the requests I will now admit were obscure, but without the library staff's help we could not have presented such fact-filled pages.

Of course, the book staff would have had nothing to work with had it not been for the team of JetCapade journalists who traveled the world from January to September 1988. Key members on that team were:

David Mazzarella, president of *USA Today* International and JetCapade director, coordinated JetCapade on the road and was the key person in arranging interviews with national leaders. He also assisted in editing this book.

Ken Paulson, my chief of staff and JetCapade managing editor and now executive editor of *Florida Today,* began planning JetCapade in September 1987. He recruited the staff and directed newsgathering efforts. He was involved in some of the early discussions regarding this book.

John M. Simpson assisted in planning JetCapade and served as the advance team editor during the trip. Simpson, who is now managing editor of *USA Today*'s international edition, also helped with the final manuscript.

Other primary players were:

Mary Ellin Barrett, reporter; Kathleen Smith Barry, photographer; Ramon Bracamontes, reporter; Stephanie Castillo, reporter; Liz Dufour, photographer; Gaynelle Evans, reporter; Tom Fenton, reporter; Mireille Grangenois Gates, reporter; Marilyn

Greene, reporter; Gwenda Iyechad, reporter; Laurence Jolidon, reporter; Don Kirk, reporter.

Also Paul Leavitt, reporter; Kevin T. McGee, reporter; Martha T. Moore, reporter; William Nicholson, reporter; Larry Nylund, photographer; Dan Neuharth, reporter; John Omicinski, reporter; Bill Ringle, reporter; Joel Salcido, photographer; Callie Shell, photographer; and Catherine Shen, reporter.

Another team of editors, reporters, photographers, and researchers conducted town meetings in Japan and Germany, which provided information for key sections of this book. They include: H. Darr Beiser, Ben Brown, Michelle Healy, Karen Jurgensen, Denise Kalette, Carol Knopes, Julia Lawlor, Joan Murphy, Jim Norman, Gene Policinski, and Darcy Reid Trick. Other reporters and correspondents filled in on a special assignment basis, especially Allen F. Richardson in London, Bill Scott in Rome, Ted Iliff in Munich, Alan Robinson in Mexico City, Marina Specht in Madrid, and Dan Newland in Buenos Aires.

Special thanks goes to Chris Wells, who handled the painstaking, day-to-day logistics of the JetCapade trip.

Also, for their support throughout JetCapade, as well as during the writing of this book, much appreciation goes to Gannett Chairman, President and Chief Executive Officer John Curley; *USA Today* Editor-in-Chief John C. Quinn; *USA Today* Editor Peter Prichard; *USA Today* Executive Editor Ron Martin; *USA Today* Editorial Director John Seigenthaler; *USA Today* Publisher Cathleen Black; *USA Today* President Thomas Curley; Gannett Vice President/News Services Nancy Woodhull; Gannett Vice President/News Charles Overby; and Gannett Vice President/Public Affairs and Government Relations Mimi Feller.

Finally, thanks to the publishing people at Doubleday, especially editor Shaye Areheart.

Allen H. Neuharth